THE
CHANGE
MAKER
EFFECT

Unleash unstoppable growth in your organisation by mobilising
the right people to do the right work at the right level

JO STEEN

FOREWORD BY DR SHEILA ROSSAN, PHD, CPSYCHOL

RƎTHINK PRESS

First published in Great Britain in 2020
by Rethink Press (www.rethinkpress.com)

Cover image © Shutterstock | Vik Y

Contents

Foreword

I first met Jo in 2000 when I was training her and some of her colleagues. She was particularly taken with the Bioss philosophy and methods, and as she progressed her career we trained her staff in every organisation in which she worked.

We have been able to understand why some teams are successful whereas others are not; why what have been seen as 'personality clashes' about which one can do nothing are not that at all and can be resolved to the satisfaction of all parties; why some 'burnouts' occur and how to eliminate them.

I joined Bioss (Brunel Institute of Organisation and Social Studies) working with Gillian Stamp, who had worked with Elliott Jaques. His book *Requisite*

Organisation was the seminal book to set out an approach different from theories current at the time. Gillian had worked with him and devised 'Career Path Appreciation' (CPA), a new way of defining how an individual's career could develop, both now and in the future, in line with Jaques' theory. Gillian asked me if I could design a simpler technique to use with relatively inexperienced administrators, which we called IRIS.

IRIS uses questions that people with any kind of experience and any range and depth of knowledge can answer. The questions are open-ended, but unlike most open-ended interviews, it has a highly structured scoring system that has been shown to be exceptionally reliable and valid. Due to the semi-structured nature of the interview, people derive an enormous amount of personal benefit from their participation whilst also enjoying the process. Comments from participants support this contention.

IRIS began its life as a recruitment tool and has been used worldwide for recruitment, promotion, career development, succession planning and counselling. It has been used in North and South America, Eastern and Western Europe, Australia, New Zealand, China and the Far East. It has been conducted on CEOs and start-up entrepreneurs, white- and blue-collar workers as well as miners and disadvantaged groups with little schooling. Research in England and South Africa has shown IRIS to be gender-fair and culture-fair. IRIS interviews can also have a major impact as a manage-rial tool to diagnose potential and current problems in organisations.

IRIS has been enhanced by Jo and I in recent years. We now refer to the output of the interview as a measure of an individual's 'complexipacity', and to the inter-vention as a 'complexipacity assessment'. To improve the face validity of the assessment and to move away from the idea that it is just a recruitment tool, the enhanced version is called 'Reveal Developmental Potential' rather than IRIS.

The tool ensures that not only are the individuals' developmental potentials recognised, but also that the developmental potential of teams, groups and the organisation itself are recognised and utilised. In addi-tion it is a powerful tool to be used in social, economic and political changes that affect an organisation. These changes include issues such as economic down-turns, economic upturns, mergers and acquisitions, and untoward events that change an organisation's bottom line.

Dr Sheila Rossan, PhD and CPsychol

Introduction

Imagine that a physics graduate enters human resources. The problem-solving enthusiasm of a natural scientist is introduced to a function with interventions that lack much, if any, scientific rigour. Without an integrated frame of reference these interventions undermine each other and fail to address the problems they promise to solve.

Across the globe HR teams are busy using this myriad of well-marketed interventions. In spite of all this activity and expense, a large number of people are mismatched either to their role, their manager or both. The simple fact is that the majority of these HR interventions don't work because they are measuring the wrong thing. Imagine a finance department working with systems that don't provide valid or reliable outputs.

There had to be a better way. Determined to find it, I came across some old science which looked at how to identify and measure individual and business potential, tracked down the scientists and academics and insisted on being trained in the methodology.

Over the last twenty years I have successfully applied these learnings to large corporations, small- and medium-sized enterprises and founder-led start-ups. More recently the work has expanded to private equity firms, family offices and investors, where we have used the science to accurately predict business and investment performance, to identify the right targets for mergers and acquisitions, and to ensure that the latter are swiftly and successfully integrated.

There have been many books written about the science, but they were written for an academic rather than a business audience. *The Changemaker Effect* is an attempt to reposition this knowledge with an up-to-date and commercial approach. What is needed is an integrated system that covers talent management, organisation design, training, development and reward. This book will outline it. It works equally well in large corporations looking to transform and in start-ups looking to scale. After all, they are two sides of the same coin.

This book is aimed at:

- Early stage founders and the start-up community, including labs and incubators: start-ups are human enterprises building new products and services under conditions of extreme uncertainty. Human capital, however, is usually overlooked in favour of product, investment and technology. Scaling on stable foundations and getting it right the first time is the key to achieving high growth at pace.

- Corporate and SME CEOs, CFOs and functional leaders: the world is changing fast. We are experiencing a new normal that is digital, global and much more entrepreneurial. Legacy corporations will require revolution not evolution if they are to survive, with human capital leading the charge at an organisation level not just from HR. Like the phoenix rising from the ashes they will need to emerge stronger, smarter and more powerful.

- HR directors, managers and would-be managers.

- Private equity partners, family offices and investors.

- Political and government leaders.

- MBA and CIPD students, HR undergraduates, management consultants and academics looking for a proven, science-based model to underpin their human capital work and education.

- Anyone who wants to better understand their work experience and use this knowledge to navigate their own development journey.

Once you have read this book you will:

- Discover a new word and phenomenon, that of 'complexipacity'.

- Understand how to use human capital to build resilient, resourceful organisations and institutions that can withstand unforeseen crises and natural disasters.

- Understand that the capability of the CEO and the leadership team is the single biggest predictor of future business and investment performance.

- Learn how to identify and champion 'changemakers' to create competitive advantage. These individuals are capable of working with high levels of complexity and uncertainty, and are scarce. They are national treasures and when found, they must be cherished, retained and, whenever possible, repatriated.

- Understand that there is no such thing as a 'problem person', and why the inordinate amount of resources spent fixating on personality are a waste.

- Understand why most performance management efforts fail and how to eliminate the need for them.

and his business partner Dr Gillian Stamp,[2] and in turn to Bioss,[3] the organisation they set up at Brunel University.

Their methodology became the bedrock of all my people management work from that point, but it was meeting Dr Sheila Rossan at Bioss and being exposed to her work that transformed my thinking and ways of working. It is Sheila who has patiently tutored me over the last twenty years and taught me the value and power of the work when used as an integrated people management system across an organisation led by line managers who know the business best, rather than HR.

Writing this book is about sharing my knowledge of the theory more widely, as Jaques himself originally intended. It is my personal interpretation of the science and it is based on my personal experiences of implementing it across corporations, small- to medium-size enterprises and start-ups. It has the power to transform current organisations and institutions and deserves to be resurrected with a modern approach.

Most assessment methodology, and the focus of most head-hunters and internal talent managers, is on skills, knowledge, experience and personality.

---

2   Gillian Stamp and Bioss International, 'A Summary of Stratified Systems Theory', Bioss International, 1985. Other papers and articles can be found at www.bioss.com
3   www.bioss.com

Despite lengthy and often expensive hiring processes, individuals continue to fail.

'Complexipacity' is the missing piece of the puzzle and a complexipacity assessment is the critical missing piece of any assessment process. The term was first referenced in 2010 in articles by both David Pearce Snyder[4] and Dr Rossan in a special issue of the journal *On the Horizon* (Vol 18:1) on complexipacity.[5] Put simply, what the science explains is that our ability to handle complexity grows with age. It grows at a predictive rate, but more significantly, it grows at different rates in different people. It is complexipacity, defined as 'our capacity to handle complexity', that underpins most of the problems in organisations and is the piece that is missed or missing by those working in the fields of talent management, job evaluation, training and development and reward.

As roles become more senior, they bring with them considerable complexity, ambiguity, unpredictability and risk. There are also more options and stakeholders to manage. If an individual is unable to cope with the complexity of the decision making and problem solving required in a role then no amount of skills, knowledge, prior experience or hard work can compensate. Ironically, leaving someone in a role where there is a complexipacity mismatch is the worst thing

---

4   D Pearce Snyder, '"Complexipacity" What is it? Do we need it? Can we get it?', *On The Horizon*, 2010, Vol 18 No 1
5   Sheila Rossan, 'The capability of young people', *On the Horizon*, 2010, Vol 18 No 1, pp71–78

to do, but it is what usually happens in the hope that time will be the healer. Unfortunately, given more time, things always get worse and a delay in acting usually has serious consequences for the organisation, for the individuals, for their families and for the teams working for them.

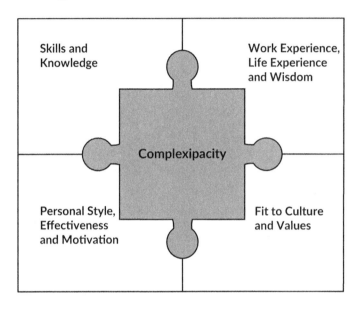

The Jigsaw of Potential. Adapted from © *bioss*

The minefield called personality, or 'personal style', needs an important mention. Leadership is much less about charisma and much more about creating a loyal following through effective and timely decision making. Unfortunately, companies spend an inordinate amount of time and resources trying to deal with the personality issue. By focusing on personality traits rather than on complexipacity, the really talented are often overlooked.

Where a person is failing in a role, a look at their complexipacity is far more useful than completing a personality assessment, assigning expensive coaches, resorting to performance management or completing 360-feedback. Indecision, poor decision making or poor management behaviour is usually a sign of a problem with an individual's complexipacity when matched to their role rather than a problem with their personality, but as complexipacity is essentially invisible and not widely understood it's the visible personality traits that are incorrectly focused on and treated.

The science allows organisations to identify their younger, internal 'changemakers', allowing them to be stretched and retained. More commonly referred to as 'high potentials', these changemakers are future business leaders. My advice is to hire externally only when you are certain no-one exists internally and if you are looking for top talent, ensure that the head-hunter of choice and their researchers are also top talent themselves.

An awareness of complexipacity also challenges conventional thinking in terms of general education bias. While proud of my physics degree it should not be confused with or used to determine potential. A first-class degree student from Oxford or Cambridge may also be a changemaker but it is not the former that guarantees the latter. University is simply the study of known knowledge, usually a great life experience and still a privilege not widely available to all. Society, governments, head-hunters and most organisations place a disproportionate importance on academic success and a university education. This is a major problem and something that needs to be better understood, particularly in light of the costs of further education.

It is interesting that many successful entrepreneurs tend not to have done well in school, and avoid university altogether due to an inability to get along with rules and rote-learning methods. In the worst cases, they exit formal education lacking any trust or confidence in it as their cognitive differences have been crushed rather than nurtured, by parents and teachers with less long-term potential than themselves.

IQ tests and aptitude tests can only be successfully completed if you have been educated and you are familiar with tests. It is possible to have a low IQ as a result of a lack of education yet have a high level of complexipacity. A complexipacity assessment is a semi-structured interview based on experiences rather than knowledge, which has to be learned. For example, South Africa and India in particular have successfully used this assessment to find highly capable people with little or no education who have been seriously suppressed and disadvantaged and, together with appropriate training, have seen numerous individuals develop and grow.

A shift to assessment of talent using complexipacity as the primary filter will always uncover overlooked talent. Prioritising cognitive capacity over skills, knowledge and prior experience (all of which can be acquired and developed) represents the ultimate diversity tool transcending any bias based on gender, religion, age, education or culture, conscious or unconscious.

If we move on to the concept that our ability to handle complexity and ambiguity grows with age, we start to get to the heart of the real problems in business today.

When the complexity of a role is well matched to the complexipacity level of an individual, we have the optimal 'in flow' situation. Individuals are energised and at ease in their roles, feeling neither overstretched nor underutilised. Decision making will be timely, and judgement calls made will be sound. Finding a flow scenario for every employee is the utopia of true employee engagement, assuming that the organisational culture is a fit and the pay is fair. A fully engaged workforce capable of timely and effective commercial decision making in turn translates into a real competitive advantage.

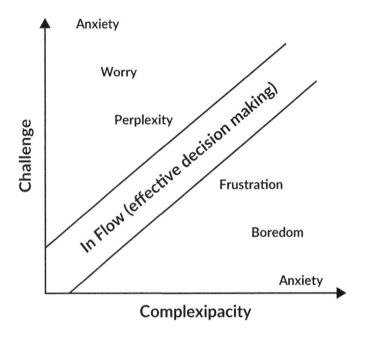

How individuals experience work. Gillian Stamp © *bioss*, adapted from M Csikszentmihalyi, *Beyond Boredom and Anxiety* (Jossey-Bass Inc, 1975). All rights reserved © *bioss*

But life in corporations, SMEs and start-ups is far from optimal, with a significant proportion of individuals, in my experience, mismatched to either their job or their manager. This manifests itself in poor overall engagement levels and disappointing financial performance. In simplistic terms, there are generally two major places where this mismatch causes problems: the first exists within the operational teams and the second is a phenomenon played out widely across leadership teams.

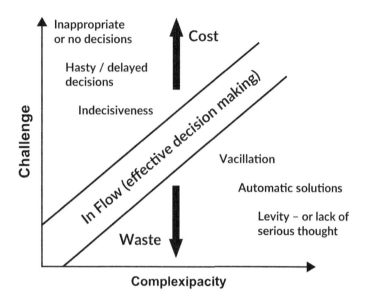

Effective decision making in organisations. Gillian Stamp ©
bioss, adapted from M Csikszentmihalyi, *Beyond Boredom
and Anxiety* (Jossey-Bass Inc, 1975). All rights reserved ©
bioss

The 'one size fits all' approach

With operational roles, talent management processes
don't take account of complexipacity and everyone's
differing ability to handle complexity. The development of operational staff in larger organisations usually
follows a 'one size fits all' approach and therefore is
paced far too slowly for changemakers. As a result,
the organisation's top talent gets bored quickly. They

may be using their spare complexipacity on outside interests when it could be put to better use within the organisation, or perhaps using it to challenge the status quo, often leading them to be erroneously labelled as troublemakers. The end result is usually that this talent leaves. Even where boredom is accurately diagnosed, the result is frequently to increase the volume rather than complexity of work, and the person still leaves. The same organisation then declares a genuine lack of leadership talent and is forced to resort to expensive and risky external hires. This downward spiral replicates like a virus, with the organisation totally oblivious to this haemorrhaging of top talent.

Boredom isn't just a changemaker problem though, and the concept of complexipacity growing with age clearly explains why someone who has been a high performer over time 'goes off the boil'. It happens consistently in the large multi-site businesses where a high performing manager is expected to continue to perform ad-infinitum. Recognising that everyone is different and that there is never a static scenario is the key. Additional complexity can be added to roles in many ways and is a powerful management tool. Use of projects and troubleshooting assignments are great ways to add complexity and keep up engagement levels in a current role if promotion is not an immediate option. Finding new business for the organisation or completing community work on behalf of the organisation can be other options.

The problem with boredom isn't just one of staff turnover. At an organisational level it results in poor decision making where individuals cannot be bothered to give a problem sufficient thought, attention or focus. On an individual level there is the impact on self-esteem and mental wellbeing through feeling underwhelmed and undervalued. Complexipacity assessments should be part of all development and assessment interventions, and they need to happen early on with promising changemakers if they are to be retained.

There is a caveat. While organisations need to look for their changemaker recruits, they must also employ and value those individuals with more modest potential. These are the people that carry the culture, that interact with customers on a day-to-day basis and are the brand's ambassadors.

The pitfalls of overpromotion

At the leadership levels in organisations the problem is a different one. It is often one of overpromotion, where the complexity of the decision making required of the role is greater than the individual can cope with. Boredom is generally easy to spot and individuals finding themselves in this place tend to be quite noisy and vocal about it. By contrast, leaders finding themselves in over their heads generally recognise this but go to great lengths to find coping mechanisms to conceal it from others. Failure to understand and assess for complexipacity when recruiting for leadership roles has serious consequences and guarantees a thriving 'Peter Principle' phenomenon: Laurence J Peter refers to people being promoted until 'they reach their level of incompetence'.[6] An old adage but still true today.

The problem starts if the promotion to a more senior role is assessed only on high performance at the level below, or if it is a result of a combination of performance together with other psychometric interventions (which, as explained earlier, are focused on the wrong things). At the heart of the science is the indication that while complexipacity grows with age, albeit at different rates in different people, everyone has a maximum level of complexipacity or a ceiling, and it is at this level that they will ultimately do their best work. Promotion beyond this level should be avoided at all costs by both the organisation and the individual.

In the absence of an understanding of complexipacity, and in the belief that we are all equal, promotions are rarely passed up, particularly when they come with additional salaries, benefits and status. Overpromotion is a world where individuals are overwhelmed and unable to 'see the wood for the trees', a world of anxiety and stress for themselves, their families and their teams. The individuals generally know that they

---

6   Laurence J Peter and Raymond Hull, *The Peter Principle* (William Morrow & Co Inc, 1969)

are out of their depth but don't know why. They work harder in the hope that this will solve the problem, they withdraw or they redraw the role to match what they can handle and give someone else the work they cannot do.

Pride, status and the problem of personal expenditure always rising to meet a new salary means admitting there is an issue is rarely an option for senior staff. Warning signs to look out for can include poor decision making, a lack of timely decision making, repeated requests for more data (hoping that this will ultimately provide the answer), the statement 'I don't know but I'll know it when I see it...', delegation of their work to direct reports, micromanagement of direct reports, or actually doing the work of their direct reports because it is more comfortable than their own.

Individuals who were high performers at the level below suddenly go from 'hero to zero'. Where individuals are a good fit to the culture, they often die a slow death. The organisation grants them more time to perform, which is the last thing they need, until they are eventually replaced. Great performers are unnecessarily lost from the organisation and individuals who loved working for the organisation suddenly find themselves marginalised and searching for new roles. Ironically, this is usually at the level at which they have just failed, and their careers rarely recover.

If one thing can be achieved by highlighting the significance of complexipacity it would be to make it acceptable for leaders to put their hands up when they realise they have been overpromoted and for organisations to allow them to be repositioned and returned to the level at which they were happy and did their best work. Perhaps their salary can be red circled, or an agreement reached for a gradual reduction over time, recognising that the organisation is ultimately responsible. If this could be achieved many careers could be saved, vital organisational knowledge retained and the associated trauma to both the individual and to the business avoided.

When completing a complexipacity assessment as part of an outplacement or career transition assignment I have met many people who wished their organisation had been more aware of this knowledge. With the benefit of hindsight, they wish they could wind the clock back and turn down that great promotion which became a nightmare. After all, the additional trappings of extra salary and additional benefits are only attractive in service and count for nothing once an individual is exited from an organisation.

A better understanding of the science by employment lawyers and tribunals could see repositioning actively considered as an option rather than performance management, an expensive compromise agreement or the stressful and even more expensive route of litigation. Performance management processes exist to improve performance, but they become futile and unnecessarily time consuming if the issue is one of complexipacity.

The remaining chapters address the theory in detail with a commercial spin and outline the steps an organisation should follow to identify, deploy, develop and unleash its human capital in order to maximise its potential and financial returns. Following these steps in the correct order will guarantee that The Changemaker Effect can be triggered in your organisation.

2
Always Start With Organisation Design

Whether employing staff on a permanent, temporary, interim or freelance basis, a great organisation design is the first step to ensuring that this talent can thrive. Eliminating unnecessary, non-value-adding layers and ensuring optimal spans of control will increase an organisation's pace and speed of decision making. Overhead costs will be reduced, which should make the case for starting with a good design compelling indeed.

The trouble is that the concept of structure can be negatively perceived as dull, serious, hierarchical, bureaucratic, authoritarian, old-fashioned and somehow no longer that important. This is particularly the case with entrepreneurs, who often like to construct organisations devoid of any structure in the mistaken belief that flat structures, ambiguous reporting relationships and chaos are somehow more modern and 'cool'. This chapter makes the case for why structure and hierarchy is absolutely necessary and why it is always the first step in The Changemaker Effect.

In general, corporations have too many layers at both the strategic and operational levels. By contrast, startups often do not have enough as they mature and evolve. Good people in a poorly designed organisation will be sub-optimal at best, or fail and leave at worst.

Starting with an understanding of the work before matching a role or person to that work is key, but organisation design must not be confused with job evaluation. Most systems of job evaluation are too subjective and do not work. Their flawed emphasis on numbers of direct reports and budgets rather than the complexity of the work itself is the reason why we have so much dysfunctionality, frustration and confusion in organisations today. In addition, the outputs of job evaluation or grades that relate to pay often morph into reporting lines.

To overcome any negativity towards hierarchy, think about the different layers in an organisation as being required to handle the increasing complexity of the work rather than for any reasons of power, authority or control. In a global organisation, there is considerable complexity at the highest levels. Hierarchy is necessary for problem solving, to establish effective relationships with people both within and outside of the company, for effective communication and translation, and for the setting of clear accountabilities.

Another way of positioning the need for hierarchy is to look at it in terms of basic physics. The more energy that is efficiently transferred from the leadership team to those actually doing the day-to-day work, the more powerful the organisation and the more likely it is to thrive. A successful organisation can never depend on just one person at the top. These are celebrity or hero CEOs who can only hope to maximise short-term shareholder value.

Jaques was the original pioneer in this field, and although it has been developed further by the organisation he set up, it has not gained any real kind of mass momentum. Other organisations have emerged with tools that lack scientific rigour, which explains why so many fads and initiatives rolled out by HR departments, consultants and consultancies fail to stand any test of time.

What the science tells us is that in the world of work there are only seven different types, or domains, of work. While Jaques and Stamp referenced work 'levels',[7] Sheila Rossan and I prefer to talk about work 'domains' as all work adds value and we feel that the

---

7   Jaques, *Requisite Organisation* and www.bioss.com

word 'levels' suggest an ordering with an associated notion of prestige, superiority and 'goodness'.

The concept of domains is that each has at least one area of expertise. The people working within that domain 'own' that expertise and are rewarded for it. We must recognise the importance and value of both work and people throughout an organisation.

The domains include all aspects of business from frontline work to the work of CEOs of global businesses and institutions. Each domain of work has its own form of mental processing and approach to problem solving. Each also has an associated 'time horizon' which guides us as to how far into the future an individual in that domain is likely to be able to see, and also what time lag there may be between a judgement call being made and the ability to see the results of that judgement. The more complex the work, the longer the time horizon will be. An additional management layer must add value and is only justified if it requires a more complex level of thinking and a longer time horizon for making decisions.

In the most complex global entities there should be a maximum of six layers of management supporting and adding value to the frontline – one populating each of the work domains. Thinking of the domains as a support hierarchy helps to demonstrate how one domain adds value to the next, with the customer the ultimate beneficiary. A support hierarchy also highlights that each domain, with greater complexity and a longer time horizon for outcomes to appear, assists the domain with less complexity and the shorter time horizon.

Six layers may be impossible operationally, perhaps the business trades seven days a week or has extended trading hours, but in the event that there is more than one management layer per work domain there will always be a consequence. The key is to understand these consequences and organise by taking them into account. The nuances of getting this balance right will be addressed in Chapter Six.

Head offices are a different matter and there should be no excuse for over-layering. The great irony is that organisational cost-cutting usually takes place within the operational domains of an organisation where the work hasn't gone away, placing unnecessary pressure on staff. By contrast, much greater savings could be made by taking out the unnecessary and often flabby senior- and middle-management layers without anybody noticing any detriment. Ironically, taking out these unnecessary layers always makes things better, not worse, enabling more to be achieved with less.

The seven work domains

This next section gives a detailed explanation of each of the seven domains of work so that you can start to apply this model to your own organisation.

Work domain: Judgement within routine

This is the work of frontline brand ambassadors creating value for customers. The work is largely prescribed with defined outputs. Individuals are accountable for the efficient use of their own time and any equipment and systems they use to do their jobs. They will have the technical knowledge for the area in which they are working. The problems faced are concrete 'real world' problems that are largely familiar and repetitive but nevertheless call for some judgement. Guidelines or procedures may be available to help with problems. Changes are likely to be driven by the other domains. Individuals will be accountable for adapting to change and making suggestions for improvement to their manager.

It may take anything from minutes, days or up to three months before there is sufficient information to make it clear that there is a problem with the quality of this work. If there is a problem with the work completed in this domain there will be considerable consequence for an organisation's reputation and its long-term viability. While this work is being increasingly automated, the inability of a computer to make judgement calls and build human relationships make interesting considerations.

Examples: frontline operators, service providers and tradesmen.

Work domain: Judgement outside routine

Work in this domain can no longer be described solely in terms of procedures or routines. New situations need to be analysed and judged, with alternatives considered before deciding on a course of action. Individuals will be expected to implement changes in their area and to recommend changes to processes, procedures or routines to their manager. It will be more than three months before sufficient messages are received from the external and internal worlds to diagnose underperformance.

Examples: first-line managers or supervisors (where individuals have control over people and processes but no accountability for a budget) and specialists.

Driven by the salaries they are prepared to pay, many multi-site organisations position their unit managers in this domain, with considerable consequence. By contrast, leading service providers position their frontline here, providing more scope for empowered decision making.

Work domain: Management of systems

The work of this domain is about best practice. It involves responsibility for the continuous improvement of an organisational unit that includes a set of people, equipment, premises and accountability for a budget. Practices and systems need to be introduced to support production or service, to contain costs, to realise purpose and to enhance reputation. Creating links between the organisational unit and the local community in which it operates is vital. The focus is on the present with some contribution to the future, which involves fine-tuning systems and being consulted on, or involved in, developing policy and strategy. Accountability for execution and the management of change sits firmly within this domain. It can be more than a year before the fruits of some decisions made in this domain can be seen and the quality of judgements evaluated.

Examples: department/unit managers and senior specialists.

In multi-site businesses, positioning the unit management role in this domain generates a more empowered and engaged operation. This approach also requires less oversight and co-ordination, reducing the need for and the significant overhead costs of additional non-value-adding management layers.

Work domain: Future orientation (functional)

This is the first domain that looks beyond where we are now and focuses on where we need to be. The essence of the work is to develop strategies to bring into being those products, services, outside relationships, structures and systems that are required for the organisation to continue to be viable and competitive in changing social and business environments.

Abstract and conceptual analysis is needed to identify problems and develop likely future solutions. These solutions are often less than concrete and have to be mentally modelled before being put into effect. Since tomorrow's solution may not yet exist, the individuals need to be able to conceptually grasp the causes of problems identified by their direct reports. This often requires the ability to convince others to accept abstract solutions before they have been proven. Accountability is now for driving rather than managing change. Events need to be controlled and influenced and change needs to be anticipated and planned for using a breadth and depth of business knowledge, experience and networks.

Specialist work is focused on designing and developing new systems, services, etc to support a particular function or in response to an aspect of the outside world, such as the market, or a change in regulatory conditions.

It can be at least two years before some judgements made at this level can be seen and evaluated.

Examples: functional leaders in a national business and strategic specialists.

Transition from direct operational management to strategic leadership is where a high level of error occurs if promotion is based solely on great operational performance and ignores an individual's complexipacity. Great performance in any domain may suggest that this is where the person does his or her best work and so should not be moved upwards.

Work domain: Future orientation (national)

This work involves ensuring the external and internal viability of an enterprise as a financial and social entity. This involves guiding the organisation through all aspects of its interactions with commercial, economic, political and social environments.

A CEO or president at this level, where the business is either domestic or a national business unit within an international organisation, will do this by:

- Providing a view of the strategic unit as a financial entity – as a business.

- Providing a view of the business as a social entity – with a reputation, a culture appropriate to the country and a responsibility to its communities.

- Providing a climate for some projects where the fruits will not be immediately seen, eg long-term alliances.

- Being alert to early indications of new opportunities for business and market presence.

Specialist work is focused on creating new knowledge that goes beyond any already defined field, is not expected to have immediate application but is expected to add value in time.

It can be at least five years before some judgements made at this level can be seen and evaluated.

Examples: CEO or president of a national business or international subsidiary, functional leaders in an international business, and strategic specialists.

Only a small percentage of the population is capable of leading a national business and so it is often the case that businesses are led in error from the functional work domain. In this case, the CEO or president still only has a functional perspective and is unable to join all the dots required for full and successful integration. They lack sufficient breadth of vision and time horizon for decisions essential at a company level. They simply can't see far enough ahead to anticipate what is likely to happen. Overvaluing sociability rather than abstract thinking also compounds poor selection at this level.

Work domain: Future orientation (international)

This work involves creating and sustaining a climate to protect strategic units, embedding them in host cultures and alerting them to possibilities of evolution over time. This involves networking beyond the commercial world to develop an understanding of actual and potential economic, political, technological, social and religious contexts.

A CEO at this level, where the business is international but not yet global, will do this by:

• Allocating resources and assessing their utilisation.

• Ensuring that experience and information about business relationships in other cultures and the subtle skills required to work within these are shared.

• Demonstrating in word and deed how the sum may be greater than the parts.

• 'Holding the faith' for everyone else.

• Providing a clear picture of corporate culture and an overall understanding of the extended contexts of the company.

A specialist person would provide support by:

• Scanning and monitoring the world-wide environment – both specifically relevant to the businesses and more generally.

• Developing company-wide systems for implementing principles and policies.

- Creating new knowledge/technologies with no immediately foreseeable application.

It can be ten years before some judgements made at this level can be seen and evaluated.

Examples: CEO of an international business and functional leaders of a global business.

Overpromoted executives in this domain will always struggle to grasp and respect the complexity of multiple cultures and multiple governance frameworks.

Work domain: Future orientation (global)

This work domain effectively takes the substance of international work and applies it on a global stage. These are the CEOs of only the largest super-corporations or institutions. They are largely concerned with bringing into being the context, environment or landscape for future generations of an organisation in places or with activities that may appear peripheral at the time, but will eventually be seen to have strategic advantage. These contexts might include entry to previously closed or unexplored nations and markets or to potential groupings of nations or, in an even wider landscape, the design of completely new forms of social, economic or political institutions. There is now a clear shift from strategic thinking to visionary thinking. CEOs at this level need data on potential political, demographic, environmental and cultural changes pertaining to the next one or two generations.

While the original time horizons cited for operational work still hold, the shift from the industrial to the information age has created time compression in the business cycles of the strategic future orientation roles. The ability to spot trends in data quickly and to take advantage of them rapidly is now absolutely critical. These organisations will continue to reinvent themselves, stay relevant and stay ahead.

Individuals capable of high work complexity make unusual non-linear connections with data and also see far further ahead than most. This combination, together with their thinking agility, allows them to make fast and sound judgement calls for their organisations. This is why I refer to them as treasures, and those organisations that have them and correctly place them will win. By contrast, overpromoted teams will drown in the data, act more slowly, fail to spot the right trends and make poor decisions. Blackberry's fate is a good example of this.

Advancing to the next level of work complexity is not a simple matter of gaining promotion. As we can see from this brief outline of the domains, the differences in the level of complexity and thought in the strategic domains are significant. It is not just a matter of 'more of the same' but of a different way of thinking.

All too often the complexipacity required at the top is underestimated and this, coupled with the scarcity of individuals capable of operating in the 'future orientation' domains, explains the short-term thinking of so many companies and governments today.

Management layers

The level of an organisation in terms of where the leader sits is determined by an organisation's vision, strategies, their associated timeframes and the complexity of the interactions required with the external environment. By applying the principle of one management layer per work domain, the number of layers can be established easily. In some professional services, organisations, technology-based start-ups and enlightened service providers the customer interface is achieved from the 'judgement outside routine' domain.

The consequences of having more than one management layer per domain are important to address. They are likely to provide the necessary impetus and motivation to address any anomalies and reap the associated cost benefits. Over-layering is a disease that has significant consequences for talent, innovation, creativity, pace and the 'bottom line'.

Where someone is in the same domain as their direct report, a tug of war will always result. Both individuals see the world through the same lens and possess the same capability for solving problems. In this case, the manager can only solve the problem from prior experience. If prior experience doesn't provide the answer the direct report needs to find someone with mental processing capacity at the next level to solve the problem. The boss is thus really a 'straw boss' or middleman who can only co-ordinate rather than lead and the 'real boss' then needs to be found if there is to be any chance of getting a decision. There is also the issue of prior experience becoming increasingly less relevant and potentially redundant given the pace of change.

Bypassing the formal reporting lines on a regular basis brings about tensions, while respecting them inevitably results in time wasted through indecision, bureaucracy and red tape. Ironically, in organisations that are severely over-layered, the 'real boss' may not even be at the next level but the one beyond that.

Beyond the problems of delayed decision making in over-layered scenarios, direct reports also complain of micromanagement, a sense of 'too many cooks', a feeling that their manager is breathing down their necks, interfering in their work too much, constricting their innovative ideas and, finally, that their managers are doing the direct report's work rather than their own in many cases. When it comes to reviews of performance or pay in this scenario, the direct reports have absolutely no confidence in the opinion of their manager.

In the event of missing layers, direct reports complain that their managers are too distant, hard to understand, seem impatient, expect too much and fail to provide sufficient context or detail. In these cases, managers get pulled down into current crises and often find it easier and quicker to do the work themselves. In this example, the present always drives out the future.

Even worse is the scenario where a manager has less complexipacity than their direct report, which occurs more often than you might think. This situation is a disastrous producer of stress and conflict and unless addressed will result in the disengagement and failure of the direct report. In the worst cases it can lead to the direct report doubting their own ability and, at its extreme, doubting their sanity with the associated impact on their mental health.

Effective communication is best achieved by populating each of the work domains whereby each management layer acts as a translator upwards, downwards and horizontally. Thinking of a hierarchy as necessary for effective relationships and for effective overall organisation communication to turn strategy and purpose into action can also be helpful in overcoming any perceived negativity. In an ideal scenario, strategic uncertainty is transformed into operational effectiveness through a cascade downwards and a reciprocal upward flow of information based on the current reality. An optimal manager and direct report relationship can only be established where there is one work domain separating the two.

Customers, Products, Reputation

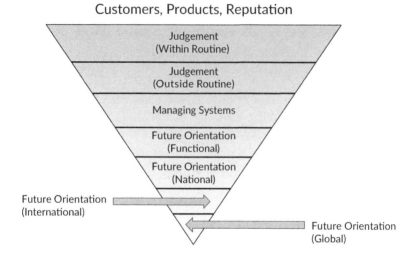

The Support Hierarchy

It is important to differentiate between the organisation design of operational units and specialist functions. In the case of the former, the management layers are primarily focused on management, with the customer interface the ultimate output and touch-point for customers. Management training for this group is vital.

Transitions from one domain to another are critical. Different work needs to be valued as individuals move from managing themselves to first-line management, to learning to manage systems, to leading a function, to leading a business unit, to managing several business units and to leading an entire global or social enterprise. Interventions for leadership development must be firmly rooted in these key leadership transitions.

It is often not the same in the case of specialist functions. The senior manager is the senior specialist as well as a manager. Work needs to be focused at the level of the most senior specialist with direct reports available at the domains below to provide support. Encouraging over-delegation of work or 'delegation disease' in the specialist functions often means that critical work is done in the wrong work domain and it therefore suffers in terms of scope and quality. This is an important and critical differentiation to understand and provide for.

Significant competitive advantage and dominance can be obtained when specialist functions are led from a more complex work domain than a competitor. This is particularly important to consider and implement as part of business strategy. Similarly, where a business is in turnaround, significant pace can be achieved by a CEO leading from a more complex work domain than would normally be required.

Having spans of control that are too small in a business is a contributing factor to the problems of over-layering. As a rule of thumb, every first-line manager must be able to know every direct report, their work performance, their ambitions, their potential, their personal circumstances and any issues that are likely to affect their work, plus they should be able to coach and train. First-line managers should oversee their direct reports' work continuously and this is the reason why attempts to make these individuals extend their reach and become dual-site managers always fails. In the case of extended trading hours additional support may be required to handle the operational and people challenges on a shift. It is important to make it clear that providing this support does not make them the line manager.

In the case of large operational units, department managers should know all team members. They should have the capacity to coach and train their direct reports and the bandwidth to have at least one quality development conversation a year with any direct reports once-removed (see Chapter Six). If everyone is working in the same place and colleagues see each other every day, this could be up to 250 people. In the case of a multi-site business a field manager may have less team members, but the number would be arrived at by applying the same principles. Setting up sound people systems in all operational units is important. Some anonymity is inevitable and accepted in the strategic domains and beyond whenever there are large numbers of frontline staff, but anonymity in the operational domains is a major problem as they should represent the foundation for high levels of morale at a unit or department level.

For start-ups it is about recognising the point at which the organisation moves from entrepreneur mode (where everyone reports to the founder) and starts to require additional layers. Clear accountabilities and key performance indicators are also needed at this point. In planning for growth, start-ups must prioritise the 'managing systems' role early on to ensure execution is covered. Ironically, it is usually this domain that is missed. All roads leading to the founder represents a single point of decision making which is not scalable, increases risk and also represents a single point of failure whereas adding necessary layers allows lean start-ups to become lean enterprises, permitting them to scale without sacrificing speed or agility and without becoming dysfunctional. Scaling on unstable foundations is a recipe for chaos and failure. I often refer to corporations as just badly scaled start-ups who have lost their founders and their sense of purpose.

The guidance on spans of control outlined above assumes that the individuals assigned to the different work domains are capable of carrying out the required level of work complexity. A mismatch will always result in more layers and smaller spans of control as this is an automatic coping and self-preservation mechanism. We will cover this in detail in the next chapter when we focus on matching the right individual to the work.

Finally, we should address matrix structures and cross-functional teams. A matrix organisation is one in which people report to multiple managers with reporting lines operating both vertically and horizontally. Individuals may report to both their line manager and also to functional leads, ie they may be held to account by different managers. The key is to understand who is accountable for what specific results. Similarly, in team scenarios the key is to establish who the designated leader is and the accountabilities of all team members. Accountabilities are deliverables rather than responsibilities, activities or tasks and cannot be delegated or shared. Without sufficient attention matrix structures can often result in management by consensus and in greater authority being held by the specialist functions than the lines of business.

3
Not Everyone Can Be The CEO

Now we understand that the more senior a role the more complexity is involved, we can look at how the science works when we start to map people to roles. The critical statement is that capacity to handle complexity differs individually. We simply do not all have the same potential.

This notion that we each have a ceiling in terms of our complexipacity is something that CEOs often find hard to reconcile because they erroneously believe everyone aspires and strives to be the boss. Experience shows that people generally have a good sense of what their ultimate potential is, or put another way, the ultimate domain of work they will be capable of in the future. Individuals who have 'ideas above their station' are in the minority and they tend to leave because either they don't get the promotions they feel they deserve, or they get them and then fail and end up leaving in a different way.

That there is a substantial range of difference between individuals and that individuals are well aware of these differences is the case in point. We are able to sense when another person is using a different mental processing capacity than ourselves. We feel either that we are encompassed by their thinking, or conversely, that we encompass theirs. It is this relativity in mental processing that is often incorrectly labelled as mystical or charismatic leadership. Charisma is a by-product of an individual working at full capacity and loving it. This generates a sense of excitement and it is this that comes across to others. In this search for the 'holy grail of charisma', organisations falsely set off to identify the special, elusive personality qualities in these people in order to present these differences in the form of competencies. The idea is that these competencies can then be assessed in others. In all instances, competency-based assessments should be replaced with complexipacity assessments and then the correct point of difference would be both assessed and understood.

Assessing people to find this ceiling and ensure that no-one is 'Peter Principled' and that all are developed in line with their own personal capacity could be viewed as 'labelling' people. But why would we want to overpromote someone and have them struggle and fail with all the associated consequence and distress to their teams, families and, not least, the organisation? It is an entirely avoidable phenomenon and yet it is being played out across organisations where it is generally a given that no-one turns down a promotion.

CEOs have HR functions that routinely complete succession planning exercises identifying future potential using nine box grids or the like. Ask on what basis this succession planning exercise and labelling has occurred beyond performance metrics and there is rarely any scientific rigour to the answer. Many claim to have, and indeed sell, interventions that can determine potential, but probe for the validity and reliability behind their findings and the results are likely to be disappointing. The general lack of analytical, data-driven capabilities within HR allows these interventions to survive. Cognitive science has the answer and, frustratingly, it has had for some considerable time.

There are many books written that outline how to spot the problems of overpromotion, in effect agreeing with Laurence J Peter that the 'Peter Principle' has to be created in order to diagnose it.[8] Other books claim to be able to educate managers in terms of what work to value and what time horizons to focus on in order for them to succeed. The latter approach is fundamentally flawed. Education cannot enable someone to

---

8   Laurence J Peter and Raymond Hull, *The Peter Principle*

operate at a more complex level than they are innately equipped for in terms of mental processing.

The problem with diagnosis after the event or after the promotion is that considerable time will be wasted with a wrong hire. Initially the individual is always given the benefit of the doubt and mistakes blamed on the previous incumbent. Usually a wrong hire can get away with this for a full budget cycle or until they start to anniversary their own numbers. By the time the mistake becomes obvious considerable time has been wasted, talented direct reports have left, the business will have undoubtedly suffered, and the hiring manager's credibility lost. In the case of a recent merger, the appointment of the wrong CEO cost a family office a minimum of £12 million over a twelve-month period before matters came to a head.

I have explained why using performance as the only basis of establishing potential ensures that people are routinely promoted into roles with an inherent complexity beyond what they can handle. In some cases, they will never be capable of the added complexity while in other cases they have been given their promotion opportunity too soon. The latter is common and, as a consequence, talented individual careers are damaged unnecessarily, often forever. Faced with being exited they fail to learn, continue to pitch themselves at the wrong level and, unsurprisingly, continue to fail.

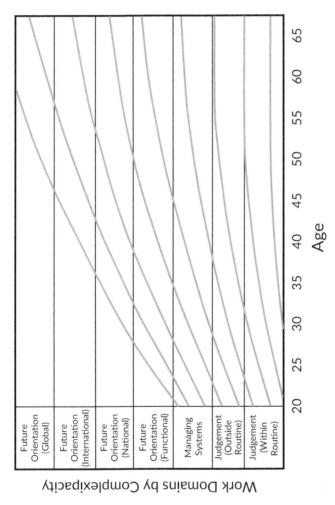

Cognitive development curves over a lifetime. Adapted from © bioss, Growth Curves © E. Jaques

The notion of individual capability is underpinned by a series of developmental or growth curves. The steeper the developmental curve, the greater the potential for complex thinking over time. It is not a question of any one developmental curve being any better than the other, but simply a question of matching the complexity of the work to the complexity that an individual can handle to ensure a 'flow' scenario to benefit both the individual and the organisation.

Rather than considering the concept of predetermined developmental curves as in any way restrictive, I would encourage CEOs to focus on using the science to assemble the right leadership team, identify their future business leaders, and at the same time create stable, customer-facing brand ambassadors on the frontline.

At first glance, observing the science challenges much conventional wisdom when it comes to talent. For example:

- Why do we retire our capable executives when their ability to handle complexity continues to grow with age? This is an interesting consideration given that this imposed 'cut-off' does not exist in other cultures. Indeed, by not retiring these highly capable executives, other cultures derive significant competitive advantage.

- Why are we fixated with youth when it comes to appointing CEOs when only those on the steep developmental curves will be capable of strategic work at a young age? It is precisely this problem that accounts for so many failures at CEO level and the associated failures of the businesses they lead.

- Investors often favour younger entrepreneurs in the mistaken belief that they have more energy and are less distracted, with fewer family responsibilities. Older entrepreneurs with high-order cognitive capability continue to have insatiable energy levels into old age and are able to translate this into better work given their more reliable strategic judgement.

- As everyone is not the same, developing frontline staff along the same timelines with a 'one size fits all' development programme is fundamentally flawed.

- Top talent needs considerable stretch and acceleration through the early work domains. Organisations generally have all the future leadership talent they need for future succession, but through mismanagement it is usually always lost.

- Succession planning usually kicks in far too late for changemakers.

Our ability to handle complexity matures in each of us along a predetermined path, regardless of gender, colour, race, ethnic or cultural background. This makes looking at talent through the lens of complexipacity the ultimate diversity tool. Bias, prejudice and stereotyping can be immediately challenged. This maturation in complexipacity is strong enough to override all but massive catastrophic life events and occurs regardless of education or work opportunity. This provides a different perspective with which to define and consider talent. We will come back to this in later chapters.

The core problem is that our ability to handle complexity is largely invisible as it is the patterning and ordering of data and information that goes on in our heads. My recommendation is always to complete complexipacity assessments on everyone. At the operational domains, the expression of complexity is sometimes hidden or identified in a negative way. Given that the cost of failure is huge in both business and human capital terms, the returns far outweigh any costs. Ideally, I would advocate training line managers so that the assessment can just form part of an organisation's interviewing process, with the substantial benefits to an organisation's reputation that follows.

As the pace of change in business shows no signs of abating, the development curves are also of vital importance when it comes to ensuring change in business. This is because, simply put, some developmental curves are more responsive to change than others.

Change or transformation in business does not require expensive change management programmes or external consultancy support, it just requires change-makers in all strategic future orientation roles and a higher proportion of changemakers to operators in the department head population.

Many organisations talk about the resistance to change in the middle-management layers leading to the often-used term 'the concrete layer'. In the case of start-ups, it is frequently for this reason that they avoid hiring any at all, which is a mistake. This phenomenon occurs where this middle-management is made up of a higher percentage of operators. Even where changemakers exist in this level, if they find themselves in the minority their views can be out-voted and change therefore resisted.

How do we go about understanding these differences? In the first instance, we can consider time horizons as a data source. When assigning projects to direct reports, managers will have a good sense of what time frames they are confident to assign. Someone working in the 'managing systems' domain, for example, should be capable of handling a project with a one- to two-year timeframe. An overpromoted manager will need to have the same single project broken down into discrete mini-projects with shorter timeframes – each one to be finished before allocating the next.

Work domains identifiable by language patterns

As part of his original pioneering scientific research, Jaques also identified differences in language patterns by work domain.[9] Specifically, he studied how we make our case when debating issues that we feel passionate about. It has to be free speech rather than in any way rehearsed or pre-prepared.

The science confirms that there are only four types of mental processing which people rely on to explain their position on a given matter. Further, these processing patterns recur at increased levels of complexity.

As a rule of thumb, when an individual is engrossed in argument, you should focus on the pattern of the argument rather than the facts themselves and consider his or her reasoning in the following terms:

- Someone capable of 'judgement within routine' work will explain his or her position by bringing forward a number of unconnected reasons to support it. Their pattern of speech will contain the words 'or/or'.

- Those capable of 'judgement outside routine' work will explain their position by bringing together a number of different ideas, none of

---

9   Elliott Jaques and Kathryn Cason, *Human Capability: A study of individual potential and its objective evaluation* (Ashgate Publishing Ltd, 1994)

which alone will make the case, but considered together they do. The language used is that of 'and/and'.

- Individuals capable of 'managing systems' work will construct their position by creating a line of thought made up of a sequence of reasons, each one of which leads on to the next, creating a chain of lined reasons, ie 'So I would do X because it would lead to Y, and Y will lead to Z…' These individuals are serial processing and the language used is 'if/then'.

- Those capable of 'future orientation functional' work will explain their position by examining a number of different positions of logic, all arrived at through serial linear processing. The several lines of thought are held in parallel and can be linked. These individuals are parallel processing and the language used is 'if and only if'.

These individuals are able to carry out all the activities necessary to manage day-to-day work from the frontline to functional leadership.

Correct placement in the 'functional' domain is vital. These individuals are able to understand and appreciate the abstract concepts of the domains above while also still being very much in touch with their operational teams. They provide the vital pivot between strategy and execution.

Beyond functional work we move into the realm of using abstract or conceptual ideas that are non-linear as a means of overcoming problems. Individuals correctly assigned to these hugely complex roles are considered in some way out of touch with reality, and to be fair, it is often the case that they are. It is important that these individuals are valued for their capacity for significant complex thinking, as they will create competitive advantage for their organisations. More than often though, they are overlooked as a result of these differences leading to functions and businesses being led by the wrong people and from the wrong work domain.

In these more abstract domains, the words used in argument are a repeat of those already explained but the reasoning is based on abstract reasoning rather than concrete: The 'future orientation: national' domain uses 'or/or'; the 'future orientation: international' domain uses 'and/and' and the 'future orientation: global' domain uses 'if/then'.

A common challenge posed is whether these mental processing patterns can be faked. If it is an unprepared and unrehearsed discussion, then the answer is no, as it is impossible for a person to argue in a language they don't possess even if they understand the underlying science. A pre-prepared presentation would be influenced favourably or unfavourably by the level of complexipacity of the author but if it is then delivered by someone with less mental processing capacity, they would be exposed under any 'on the spot' questioning. An interesting consideration is to apply these principles to the Q&A sessions at the end of corporate trading updates and to live, unrehearsed political debates.

Transitioning domains

Finally, before we move away from the theory, I would like to address the issue of transitions from one work domain to the next. As we start to move across domains, we start to see the world differently, we start to see things with a whole new mental processing capacity and through a different lens. What seemed to make sense in our old world somehow doesn't anymore. The transition itself can therefore prove unsettling and as a result we often make major life decisions both in and out of work around these times. Indeed, the mid-life crisis has been diagnosed as the transition between the 'managing systems' and 'future orientation' work domains, given the shift from operational to strategic work is seen as the most challenging transition of all. Moving from national to international leadership is also significant as it introduces a kaleidoscope of new variables.

4
Getting The Leadership Team Right

When I first started working with the theory, I tended to get very excited about using it to identify young changemakers. The problem with starting here, of course, is that you are effectively focused on tomorrow before you have sorted out today.

Leadership is a strategic imperative, so the work has to start at the top with the leadership team. What we have to establish is whether this team is operating in the right domains when considering the organisation's strategy and vision. If the leadership team is wrong, what we can be certain of is that there will be considerable consequences occurring elsewhere in the organisation.

Getting the leadership team right quickly will save a CEO at least eighteen months in time. In addition, there is the added motivation for the wider business when a new CEO is seen to address 'the elephants in the room' which are already obvious to everyone. The organisation charts are unlikely to explain what is really going on.

The first job for the CEO is to determine in which work domain their role sits. Referencing the CEO brief, business strategy and vision should give guidance on scope and timelines. These can then be compared with the work domain descriptions in Chapter two.

As a general rule of thumb:

- For corporates, the question is whether the business is national, a national subsidiary of an international business, international or a truly global business or social enterprise.

- Start-ups will generally start in the first future orientation domain as a city-based or regional business. As they scale though, they can quickly become national or international businesses.

- SMEs will vary but are likely to be led from the first future orientation domain as a minimum.

The significance of understanding the work of the CEO is that it informs, first and foremost, how many layers are required below them and the mental processing horsepower required from the individuals populating these layers. In many cases, because of a head-hunter's preoccupation with youth, the CEO is not operating from the right work domain. This is an important point which I would encourage CEOs not to overlook. Without this understanding, a CEO who is lightweight in complexipacity terms will generally go on to under-hire people, hiring those they can comfortably manage rather than what they actually need. The whole organisation will 'sag', settling at the level of complexipacity of the CEO. The CEO will inevitably underperform and will eventually be exited.

By contrast, a CEO who is prepared to recognise their level of complexipacity can be extremely successful by doing just three things:

- Acknowledge that there is a gap in the first instance and that help will be needed on the big decisions. The decisions a national CEO makes on a day-to-day basis are likely to be a blend of functional and systems decisions, but the CEO will need to be capable of making the more complex decisions when needed.

- Ensure that a suitable mentor who is already operating in the right work domain is identified to assist with those big decisions. This could be a chairman, a non-exec member or trusted advisor outside the organisation. Meet with this mentor regularly to 'chew the fat'.

- Ensure that there is no compromise on the recruitment of the leadership team, ie hire the individuals needed rather than those that can be comfortably managed. Accept that this will lead to some lively but necessary debate.

The best example I can think of is a CEO who was smart enough to get it from the off. 'Jo,' he said, 'you and I both know I can't do this job.' The acknowledgement itself was the first step. In so doing, he understood he needed help and he quickly identified his trusted advisors, with whom he would meet regularly to debate his high-level thinking. With my help, we did not compromise on the hiring of his leadership team. The outcome was success on all fronts.

By contrast, I can think of another MD with much less humility. When I arrived, he had already assembled his team. What should have been strategic 'directors' were in fact all overpromoted operational department heads, and this large business was therefore totally reliant on the MD for strategic thinking. He did not believe he needed help from anyone despite having access to some smart group executives. Ultimately, he failed because his strategic decisions were not the right ones and having assembled a lightweight team of direct reports, he had no check and balance or safety net to tell him so.

It is vital to explore the CEO's challenge to assemble a 'fit for purpose' leadership team from both a corporation and a start-up perspective. The importance of getting the leadership team right can't be emphasised enough. Getting it right quickly gives both the CEO and the business the best chance of overall success.

Being dazzled by academic prowess is the ultimate watch-out. Unless individuals are completing a PhD and exploring new ground, a degree is about regurgitating known knowledge. The student may have high cognitive capacity, but their class of degree, MBA and university of choice is not an indicator of this. Similarly, big job titles can be misleading.

Completing a complexipacity assessment on the existing team is the only fully valid and accurate intervention, but the objective of this chapter is to give CEOs some ideas to enable them to work on the situation themselves. If the CEO is new, then information can be obtained by meeting all the existing team members. If we are looking at an existing CEO who is reappraising his team, then it is likely that this information is already known.

In an ideal world, I would always advocate that a new CEO checks out his or her leadership team before starting and before accepting advice from what could be the wrong people. When I talk leadership team, I mean all individuals down to the department heads. I would also always recommend that a CEO should do this work personally or use external support rather than relying on feedback from other team members or HR to avoid any biases.

Let's first look at the CEO of a national business. The leadership team should then be made up of functional directors doing 'future orientation' work and department managers doing 'managing systems' work. From an organisation design perspective, both work domains must be populated and the department managers should report to functional directors for effective translation and communication. I say this because often there is a temptation for some departments to report in to the CEO directly. This should be avoided for an optimal structure and for effective communication. In the same way, a CEO should always avoid wearing two hats and taking on a functional role in addition to their own. Doing so immediately removes the ability to treat all functions equally and creates immediate dysfunctionality.

The number of roles that should exist in the functional domain is a point for debate. For reasons of cost, these roles could, for example, oversee more than one function. The absolute key to the functional domain is to ensure that in every case the individuals in these roles have sufficient complexipacity for the work. They must also all be changemakers and not overpromoted operators. Their focus should always be on 'new, tomorrow and change' rather than on today, the status quo and continuous improvement.

The department heads are critical. We have already commented that the bedrock of good employee relations and business success in the here and now relies on this management layer. It is this group who are in control of the business for today. This group also has influence over the people below them and this is why the CEO must be as interested and pay as much attention to getting this layer right as the functional directors. The department head work is where 'the rubber hits the road' in larger organisations and it is this group that are seen as the face of the company to the frontline.

I often find that organisations have far too many department heads. In many cases the roles are just oversized first-line manager roles and so the organisation has a higher payroll overhead than is necessary. Too many department heads also creates bureaucracy and slows down decision making.

The department heads form the interface between the directors and the frontline, converting strategy into operational work and therefore ensuring effective execution. Where businesses complain about execution it is usually down to a problem with the work being done in this domain. The problem is either that the people in these roles are the wrong people, the strategy has not been articulated to them in a language they can understand, they haven't been sufficiently involved in the strategy and/or they don't believe in the strategy (and as a result they are executing what they believe it should be with their teams).

It is on all counts that I would strongly encourage CEOs not to ignore this population. Asking too little of this group and not involving them sufficiently is a common failing.

Changemakers vs operators

Change is a given in the current climate and the pace of this change is increasing. We need to understand the difference between changemakers and operators. In the last chapter I explained that some development curves do change, while others do not. As an absolute, everyone in the future orientation roles and above must have a 'changemaking' development curve. Where this is achieved there will be no need for change management teams or expensive strategy consultants. The board will just perform their own.

Where a business needs to move fast you should have as many changemakers in the department head population that you can find. This will ensure resonance between this group and the directors, which should ensure that they are supportive of the change agenda and will reassure their teams to collaborate and support it too.

Where there are a higher percentage of operators in the department head population, change will be slower. As already explained, the serious risk is that the operators who don't like change resist, ignore or block it – encouraging their teams to do the same. If they are in the majority, there is also the potential for them to be able to outvote the changemakers. Organisations with insufficient changemakers in the leadership team will be 'continuously improving' organisations. They may fool themselves into thinking that they are changing with the times, but instead they will be on the verge of irrelevance and extinction.

The CEO needs to arrange to meet each team member, allowing a couple of hours for each discussion, to start to explore the work domain that each individual is operating in, regardless of their current job title. I'm assuming the CEO would use the time to learn about employment and family history more generally as I am often surprised at how much more I know about individuals I assess than their own organisation does.

For the purposes of getting an initial sense of complexipacity there are a couple of questions to ask:

- Ask them to describe their job as they see it rather than just quoting their job description

- Ask them to share the problems they see and how they would fix these problems if they had the authority

The CEO should get a good sense as to what domain of work the individual is describing. Are they are talking about systems, processes and efficiencies or are they anticipating the future? What time frames are they working with? Is it one to two years, or beyond? Listen to the pattern of their reasoning: if they are serial processing 'if / then' they can handle operational work and if they are parallel processing 'if and only if' then they can handle strategic work. Finally, what are the problems that they see? If they are seeing things beyond their own remit, it is likely to suggest that they have the capability to work in a more complex domain than their current role requires.

An overpromoted director will always describe their job in terms of policies, procedures and control rather than strategy. Even if they know they should be providing a more strategic description, they can't communicate in a language they don't possess. They will concentrate on short-term issues and immediate results to the detriment of longer-term actions. They will be unable to think in the abstract and they will find difficulty in perceiving lateral linkages which have not been identified or applied before. They can't conceive a solution which does not currently exist, and they see little point in networking across the business, rarely supporting other's initiatives. Multiple tasks will always be approached one at a time rather than concurrently. Where they use the word 'strategy' believing it is the appropriate word to use, the trick is to drill down and ask them to explain what they actually mean and what would be seen as a result. This will determine whether it is an original thought or just something they have read.

By contrast, individuals capable of more will be seeing problems beyond their immediate remit that others cannot. They will be challenging existing practice and thinking 'outside the box' using abstract analysis to identify new solutions to current or anticipated problems and to address future market opportunities. They will have developed a wide-ranging network of advisors to convince leaders to take different courses of action.

There are lots of cases where directors survive by virtue of a more able direct report or the potential of others more widely. By the CEO including department heads in their review, this will become evident. Asking the department heads to describe what value their director is adding to their own work is a useful way of teasing out what is really going on.

A quick check on formal employee relations activity can also prove helpful. Where individuals are 'in over their head' they regularly instigate and resort to formal process. Often these are desperate attempts to retain control over more capable direct reports. These complexipacity clashes either result in disciplinary action instigated by the manager or a grievance raised by the direct report. By contrast, capable individuals rarely need to go formal to manage performance.

Finally, in the absence of an assessment or a one-to-one discussion there a few things a CEO can look out for when trying to differentiate between changemakers and operators:

Operators

- Are 'doers' based in the here and now. Focus is on the efficiency of the current system / model. They add value through continuous improvement. They tinker and juggle rather than consider any wholesale reform.

- Prefer the status quo and require detail. They dislike any ambiguity, risk or uncertainty and resist change.

- Where problems exist, they are quick to blame and hide behind external forces.

- Tend to overweight the need and value of experience, love to create rules and like control.

- Ideas will be introduced from previous organisations in a 'cut and paste' form as they lack the thinking agility to adapt / adjust to new contexts.

- Their heads generally stay under the parapet to avoid 'rocking the boat'. In a crisis they tend to run for the hills.

- Act swiftly but often without sufficient thought. Often considered 'fast but stupid' by changemakers.

- Don't inspire changemakers or generally see their value. They see changemakers as either dreamers who are not practical enough or troublemakers needing much more experience.

- Tend not to voluntarily move organisations.

Changemakers

- Have a helicopter quality, a sense of flair and are poor at routine work.

- Are forward thinkers and own problems. They are able to see what doesn't currently exist today and make unusual connections with data.

- See the bigger picture. They show interest and commitment to the wider business and its future beyond their function or department.

- Thrive on uncertainty and ambiguity, actively using it as a resource. They push boundaries, often orchestrate conflict, challenge the status quo, take calculated risks and where they have authority they drive change.

- Are disrupters with heads that are generally above the parapet, even when they know they may be shot.

- Acquire new skills and knowledge quickly.

- Are likely to move on quickly from one thing to another and from one organisation to another without sponsorship.

- Changemakers think first and then act decisively. They resist the rush to action. This 'thinking time' can be interpreted as 'slow and lacking energy and speed' by operators.

- Are generally supressed when managed by operators as their ideas are genuinely not seen to be good ones.

- Changemakers see operators as bureaucrats blocking innovation and overvaluing practicality.

Functional directors must all be changemakers and have the complexipacity to handle strategic, future orientation work. Department heads must all have the complexipacity to manage systems work, and where the organisation requires rapid change or is in turn-around all should be changemakers. At a minimum there must always be a higher percentage of change-makers to operators in this community.

Where there is a mismatch of capabilities within either population, communication will generally prove chal-lenging, as meetings and discussions will need to be held at the level of the lowest contributor or these individuals will be unable to keep up and the discus-sions will go over their heads.

Internal promotions are key

Repositioning overstretched talent and backfilling any gaps with internal promotions before looking externally is the key. This is particularly important for new CEOs. Creating a culture whereby externals are only hired when no internal can be identified is very powerful indeed.

Believing that people who have long service with the organisation are somehow considered to be 'dinosaurs' or 'blockers' is seriously flawed. If you have a leadership team member who has long service and who is also a changemaker, treat them like gold dust. They know everything about the organisation and they also have the thinking agility to reinvent their experience. Sadly, while candidates are well aware of what they can offer they are also painfully aware that they are likely to be overlooked on the basis that their length of service is considered somehow a detriment.

A particular client springs to mind. I was asked to assess a long-serving internal and the assessment confirmed he had grown way beyond his current role. While he agreed with my hypothesis, he was certain that the organisation would not back him, whatever support I gave him. He was right and the organisation opted for a more polished and better educated but less capable individual. The experienced internal left the business and the external failed. Lessons can be learned from this.

Many independent consultants are changemakers who derail when they fail to make the transition from operational to strategic work in an employed capacity. This is a fruitful yet ignored talent pool. This can be demonstrated by a personal challenge recently to find a group property director where I forwarded a fantastic, older, highly capable candidate. The individual got the role, smashed it out of the park and the group HRD acknowledged that had the candidate not had my sponsorship he would not even have been interviewed. The additional wisdom that comes later in life often defined as the combination of capability and humanity is also squandered when overlooking this group.

Start-ups and entrepreneurs

The problem with corporations is the overpromotion of operators and the lack of changemakers at the top to do the genuine strategy, while the problem with start-ups is the reverse. By its very nature, a start-up is generally about a gap in the market and about something new that has been identified so it is more than likely that the entrepreneur is a changemaker working at the first domain of future orientation as a minimum.

The entrepreneur then over-hires, usually at unnecessary high salaries, introducing lots of friends who are likely to be on a similar mental processing wavelength. The risk here is that everyone employed is excited about strategy and the future but there is no-one introducing and managing the systems and processes required to execute the strategy, ie no-one is doing the 'managing systems' work. Lack of attention to organisation design, and in particular to a strong team in this domain, is one of the factors that contributes to the high level of start-up failures.

Entrepreneurs have an inherent dislike of systems and procedures and this exacerbates the problem further. They need to appreciate that these systems are needed for everyone else, if not them. Alternatively, to save money they just hire young talent and these individuals are only capable of operational work. In this case, all the strategic responsibility falls to the founder. Both examples are dysfunctional and contribute to founder fatigue and burnout.

The next issue for start-ups comes as they start to scale. This usually requires an initial shift to a national business requiring the addition of a future-oriented functional team. Failing to add the additional layer is one issue, but the additional concern is that often the entrepreneur is not able to handle the complexity of the bigger CEO role and fails to recognise this. International growth requires a further shift, with yet another layer required. Unless young founders are geniuses, they will not have sufficient capability to lead a national or international business, offering another explanation as to why so many start-ups fail.

The example of a young entrepreneur comes to mind. He had successfully found himself on an accelerator programme with a great idea, passion and purpose. The 'Mentor in Residence' commissioned assessments on all thirty entrepreneurs and ahead of the work highlighted this individual as a problem child. His assessment showed that he had very rare potential but insufficient complexipacity at twenty-nine to run his company. Our recommendation was that he stepped aside, became his business' brand ambassador, and a new and experienced CEO was hired to run the business. He took on the feedback and went from failing to excite investors to raising $250,000 within a matter of months.

There are also many problems with having 'family members' in a business, whether these are blood relatives or, in the case of start-ups, members of the original team. In addition to the obvious risks of overpromotion where these family members are operationally focused, they are also often able to derail strategic efforts by non-family members given their disproportionate access to, and influence over, the CEO and/or founders. One particular start-up had an overpromoted director who was also a blood family member. As he was 'protected', the only option was to reposition him as a head of department. He would often comment on his lack of confidence in his replacement's new ideas. On the strength of this feedback, the CEO fired the replacement and things went back to square one.

Investors should always understand the complexipacity of entrepreneurs and business leaders in order to understand at what point it may be necessary to bring in a CEO with more horsepower. In the same way, I believe *Dragon's Den* would benefit from a sixth dragon to ensure that the individuals pitching have the capability to match the vision they are describing.

Empirical data from studies shows that where the complexipacity of a CEO aligns with the complexipacity of an organisation's vision, substantial profits follow.[10] Conversely, where this is misaligned, investments always spectacularly fail.

The ultimate irony here is that corporations and start-ups rarely converge, which is interesting given that each has a lot of what the other needs. If corporates are to survive in the future, they are likely to need to look to the start-up world for talent unless they start to get good at attracting and developing future business leaders of their own. Creating a blend of the two and a future world of non-corporate corporates would be interesting.

Trends suggest that in the future, there will be fewer corporations in the traditional sense, meaning the requirement to work in an office for a salary. Instead,

---

10 'Predictability of Investment Performance and the Impact of the Level of CEO's and Partners. A study of 24 companies and 6 private equity firms.' Requisite Organisation International Institute, July 2011

the view is that there will be more freelancers or 'corporations of one' and much more virtual working. If this is the case, it becomes even more important to grasp the significance of complexipacity and the importance of hierarchy. This is because effective communication, translation and the setting of clear accountabilities in a world of self-employed individuals working from home, possibly anywhere in the world, has the potential for dysfunctionality and chaos on an exponential scale. Chaos in an office can at least be supervised.

When it comes to the important consideration of the recruitment of non-executives and chairmen, non-executives must at least be in the same domain as the CEO and a chairman always one domain higher.

5
Culture Is King

After creating a great organisation design and assembling a 'fit for purpose' leadership team, we need to turn to culture next. Performance issues on the frontline are far more likely to be a result of cultural or behavioural misalignment rather than an issue of complexipacity. Alongside leadership, culture is another strategic imperative.

Culture is 'how we do things around here', or more specifically 'how we behave around here'. A strong culture is the backbone of a resilient company. By contrast, a weak culture veers from doing the right thing for the organisation to doing what is right for the individual. Assume that products and services will be copied in time, but no-one can reproduce an organisation's culture.

A poor culture fit is about people doing things differently and it is the one thing that can trump mental processing capacity. If an individual is not a culture fit their performance will always be sub-optimal. This was something that Jack Welch, CEO at General Electric, could not emphasise enough. As he put it: 'If someone is hitting their numbers but doing it counter-culture,' (ie not doing it the way we do it around here…), 'then they have to go.'[11] While this statement clearly resonates, all too often toxic high performers are not addressed, to the great anxiety of all those employees whose behaviours are aligned.

Far too often, culture is left as something mystical, something undefined and somehow just something that is left out there 'in the ether'. Sometimes it is defined by words but usually these words have no further definition. This just means that the whole concept of culture becomes highly subjective with everyone having a slightly different interpretation and description.

Given that complexipacity and culture fit are the real derailers, and we have a methodology for assessing complexipacity, how do we bring rigour to culture and why is it so necessary to do so?

Let us first address why a framework is necessary. It is primarily necessary to ensure that everyone is

---

11   Jack Welch and John A Byrne, *Jack: Straight from the Gut* (Grand Central Publishing, 2003), Chapter 9: The People Factory

clear in advance on how they are expected to behave. Secondly, it is necessary to allow managers to manage those individuals who are a poor culture fit. Despite our best efforts in recruitment we only really know whether there is a cultural match once the person starts. In addition, for established hires often strategic changes can mean shifts in culture, which can result in someone being a good fit in the past but not to the future.

The reality is that in the absence of a framework of behaviours, managers cannot performance manage based on culture fit. Challenging individuals results in a discussion which, if taken further, will inevitably lead to a grievance of some sort and the real issue never gets resolved. With the impact of the challenge resulting in a problem for the manager, you can be sure that they will not go there again. The manager simply resorts to finding other mechanisms and reasons to manage the individual. Finding them doing something wrong so they can discipline them and use the more explicitly documented disciplinary process is the usual approach but this is neither honest nor fair. Whenever I challenge managers over this notion of 'catching them doing something wrong' when the issue is really a poor culture fit I am always met with smiles and agreement. The other option that is often deployed is to extend a person's probationary period and give them more training, but if the issue is a mismatch between company and personal actions then this is a waste of time, a waste of training resources and a waste of payroll.

A framework that clearly describes what behaviours are encouraged when compared with those that are not is needed as a recruitment and performance management tool rather than a marketing initiative, and we need to create one before we start to consider organisational talent any further.

The reason I advocate assembling the leadership team first is that they need to lead any work on culture, values and behaviours. It is too important to be delegated to HR or to be arrived at by some form of group consensus. To reaffirm, defining the culture of an organisation is a key strategic and leadership imperative. Leaders must define the environment they want to build. Unlike technology or product, an organisation's culture cannot be easily or quickly replicated. 'Culture eats strategy for breakfast every time' is a phrase that has been attributed to the economist Peter Drucker (www.drucker.institute).

In fact, getting the leadership team right where all individuals are well-matched in complexipacity terms to the complexity of their roles has the biggest impact on an organisation's culture. The command and control and innovation starved cultures of large corporations are largely a function of an overpromoted board. Unable to handle the real work they should be doing (which is primarily outwardly focused), they focus on internal operational work and end up micromanaging their teams and enforcing unnecessary rules to retain control.

In turn, they then under-hire and the cycles repeat at the domains below. In addition, the lack of strategic thinking and innovation from the board often means that an organisation is struggling to get things done with outdated systems and procedures. Hard work and long hours become the order of the day, which by default become key cultural themes. All of these reasons reinforce why the leadership team must be addressed first.

Once assembled as the custodians of an organisation's culture and values, this team needs to articulate and bring these to life. These are the values that uniquely and authentically define the personality of the organisation – its 'special sauce'. All too often, values are bland and consist of the same words that exist in many other organisations, so in reality they don't really mean anything. Far from being harmless, as many assume, they are often highly destructive. Empty value statements create cynical and dispirited employees, alienate customers and undermine management credibility.

The best detailed frameworks are driven by small teams that include the CEO, some (but not necessarily all) members of the leadership team, any founders still with the company and a small number of key employees from across the work domains known to be high performers and intuitively considered by the business to be 'slam dunk' cultural fits. It is a fine balance between involving employees across the business to make it real versus a 'top-down' exercise by leaders who feel they know best. In the case of the latter, the result will always be a piece of work that is not bought into, believed or considered credible by the masses, creating automatic trust issues in the organisation.

Compiling the framework

The organisation may already have a set of values, but more often than not these are just words. In the first instance, are the words the right ones to underpin the future business strategy? Once this has been debated, the words must have a clear definition or everyone's interpretation of the words will be different, rendering them useless as a basis for guiding behaviours. In founder-led businesses they are generally an extension of the founder's personal values. Corporations could do well to reference the values of original founders as a key data source and take some time to learn the history of the organisation and its culture.

The magical part is the process of getting the words and the definitions into a behavioural framework that can be used by managers. At the point that the CEO and his smaller team have identified the words and the definitions, the work can then be opened up for help with the detailed descriptors. This enables the organisation to feel that they have contributed and the wider input into the detail is useful as the framework uses real words based on real experiences.

The behavioural framework must address both the behaviours that are to be encouraged and those to be discouraged. I see so many organisations struggle with the desire to avoid specifying negative behaviours. This lacks the understanding that for managers trying to manage an individual on the basis of culture fit, the poor behaviour has to be explicitly specified. This allows the manager to point to the behaviours required by the business and company, hence avoiding the potential risk that the individual feels their manager is somehow picking on them.

Opening up the work to the wider organisation at this point is also fun. Of course, the main purpose is to get the detailed behavioural framework, but it also creates the opportunity for early validation of the top line work and a first check for resonance. For this reason, presenting the work in draft form is always recommended. The leadership team should take the work out on the road and any temptation to delegate this should be resisted.

For some reason people always seem to find it easiest to talk about people who have not fitted in, so it is key to identify what specifically about these people meant they didn't work out, and what behaviours were observed. The more precise you can be, the more helpful this is for performance management. Repeating the exercise focusing on those exemplary employees renowned for their cultural alignment should mean you have lots of material to consider. Identify the stories which could be used to bring the values to life in a tangible way; storytelling is a powerful training tool and much more helpful than rote training.

Sign-off on the detailed frameworks is ultimately down to the CEO but it's better if this detailed work is pulled together by individuals with large line management responsibilities as they have a vested interest in getting it right. A mix of operational and HQ language is also key to ensure that one framework can exist for all. From experience, and for reasons of simplicity, I would try to create one framework for the business rather than completing frameworks for leaders too. What often happens in the sessions is that individuals will cite certain leadership behaviours as a reason why they are unable to fully live the values – taking account of these will be useful when rolling out the work.

Rollout and integration

With regards to the rollout, I would guard against a mass rollout and advocate a gentler process. Ideally, the leadership team should consider the final work and commit to actively living the values and behaviours themselves for a period of time before taking out to the department heads, for example. This way they can 'call each other out' when they see counter-culture behaviour and, assuming they are successful, it will leave them less open to criticism when rolling the work out to the department heads. The department heads should then have a similar period of time to live the behaviours as a group with the same 'callout' option before pushing out to their teams. If a three-month settling-in period for both groups is allowed it would mean a six-month phased, but likely more successful, launch.

I recall my time at an organisation which had a distinct culture which made it a very 'Marmite' organisation to work for. You either absolutely loved it or absolutely hated it. There tended to be little middle ground. The value that was the most discriminatory was 'personal modesty'. Many people challenged us on that value – struggling to understand how a sales organisation could be successful with a 'we' rather than a 'me' culture. The point was that we were successful because of that value, seeking out other organisations with a similar culture, and consequently building deep, meaningful, long-lasting and profitable relationships with these partners that stood the test of time. 'Me me me' individuals never lasted long. I distinctly recall a director with great industry experience who was well-matched in complexipacity terms struggling to get anything done despite his seniority. Culture fit invisibly trumped seniority so his work tended to be deprioritised in favour of someone who may have been less senior, but who was a better culture fit and more popular as a result. No-one could have articulated their behaviours as such – it was just an unspoken phenomenon. Exasperated as to why he could never get people to do anything for him despite being on the leadership team and failing as a result, he did not last long. He will probably recall this point in his career as a real low while I describe the same business as an absolute highlight in mine and this is why the power of culture should never be underestimated.

Having nailed your values and created a detailed framework of behaviours, they now need to be integrated into every people process, ie recruitment, performance management, promotions, development, exits and reward. From an employee's first interview to their last day of work, everyone should be constantly reminded that values form the basis of every decision the company makes. Self-selection then becomes far more likely, particularly with senior hires, avoiding costly mistakes and costly exits.

Finally, actions will always speak louder than words and therefore aligned leadership behaviour will always be a far more powerful reinforcement of values than just seeing them emblazoned on walls, T-shirts and mugs.

In the same way as I believe due diligence ahead of any investment decision should always extend beyond the financials to include human capital due diligence, specifically the capability of the leadership team, it should also always incorporate due diligence on the culture.

6
Everyone Is Talent

Employee engagement is a multi-million-pound industry and the business case for achieving improved levels of engagement are widely accepted and understood. This chapter will explain that when employee engagement is considered through the lens of complexipacity it becomes an incredibly simple equation.

Employee engagement is simply:

- Having a role where the complexity of the work is well-matched to what an individual can manage.

- Having a manager who is operating at the next level of work complexity so that problems can be solved and context set.

- Knowing there is someone who is specifically responsible for the individual's development, the manager once-removed (see later in the chapter).

- Working in a company where there is a good culture fit.

- Being paid fairly (see Chapter Nine).

Free lunches, chill-out zones, remote working, relaxed dress policies, etc are all great to have, but they will never compensate if the five issues outlined above are not present.

This chapter seeks to demonstrate the importance of getting the right frontline and first-line management teams for the purposes of overall organisational engagement and organisational 'flow'. The operational, customer-facing teams are often overlooked by leadership teams, but when considered through the lens of complexipacity some exciting opportunities emerge.

The key statement is that everyone is 'talent' or 'talented' if they are in a role where the complexity of the work is well-matched with what they can handle, and they are a culture fit.

An operational team that is 'in flow' will be energised by their work; they will make sound judgement calls and provide high levels of commitment and discretionary effort. If in turn they are also a good cultural fit, they will be great brand ambassadors. This is good for the individual, for customers and, ultimately, for shareholders and investors.

This brings us back to the point that not everyone is the same, and rather than feeling uncomfortable with this I would encourage leaders to embrace it instead. Appreciating the creativity and talent of every single employee converts into a seismic competitive advantage. Around 70% of the world population will do their best work in customer-facing roles and are happy to do so. By contrast, if everyone wanted to be a senior manager, we simply wouldn't be able to run businesses. In the main, most people have a really good sense of what their ultimate potential is. All that they ask is to be given the opportunity to exercise and fulfil this potential, and to be appreciated and valued for doing so. It is usually only senior managers who think that everyone wants to be a senior manager!

I remember testing this with a particular leader. Everyone in that business knew how fabulous the organisation's receptionist was. Everyone who visited the offices, whether an employee or a client, got the warmest of greetings and was made to feel like they were the most special visitor the organisation had ever had. Clearly this was an individual very much in flow. When asked whether she had any ambition to do her manager's job she just laughed at us. 'Why would I want to do that?' she asked. 'I get to do what I love every day in a company that I love.' The point was made. She did, however, feel that there was work to do regarding pay.

The development curves give us a sense of where someone will ultimately do their best work in work domain terms. It is not a question of whether one development curve is better than the other, but a matter of ensuring that the majority of customer-facing roles are filled by people who will do their best work and make their unique contribution in those domains. Customers are then likely to get the best service. If there is a problem in these domains, the reputation and viability of an organisation is at risk and more often than not resourcing strategies do not take account of this. Ensuring the education and skills of this group are continually attended to and developed is a further human capital strategic imperative alongside that of leadership and culture. People that are working to their full potential create stronger and more profitable organisations but also more robust communities and societies. We need to pay attention to everyone, not just those at the top.

I can think of an organisation which was extremely proud of the fact that everyone they hired was a graduate. Vast amounts of money were invested in these individuals and the graduate programme was widely celebrated and often put forward for industry recognition, yet labour turnover was 50% – meaning that over a two-year period the majority had gone. An effort was made by HR to look at why everyone was leaving, when the problem was simply that the work these graduates were being asked to do was one work domain less complex than they were capable of, so once they had learned everything they were bored. By hiring more people better matched to working with the complexities of frontline work, the graduates were then able to take on more complex assignments. Labour turnover reduced and the teams were much happier and more stable.

Another client had a similar challenge. Their resourcing strategy was disproportionately focused on undergraduate students, believing that recruiting young people was what was needed to fuel their vibrant and fun culture. Again, labour turnover was high. They put this down to the unreliability of students when the issue was more the capability of the students, who found the work boring. By looking at the resourcing challenge differently we actively wrote job adverts that described the actual work in work domain language and the culture, and we attracted a much more diverse potential workforce who valued the frontline work and wanted to stay long term. Labour turnover, recruitment costs and the merry-go-round of constantly inducting new people were all reduced.

Operational management roles

Having addressed the issue of correctly matching the work complexity to what an individual can manage, we move on to cover the importance of getting the first-line manager role right. I am often asked whether organisations should be assessing these candidates. Ideally the answer is, of course, 'yes', but experience would suggest that where the leadership team is right at the department head level they will naturally, left to their own devices, hire first-line managers or specialists who are 'big enough'. Performance issues are far more likely to be a result of a poor culture fit or, in the case of a line manager, a failure to value the work of management rather than an issue with complexipacity.

Great hiring in the department head and manager roles is important for operational success. Where these are line roles rather than specialist roles the individuals must value the actual management role, must be trained in the art of management and must actively allocate time to making themselves available.

The key to line management is to value the work and to set about building a trusted relationship with team members. A trusted two-way relationship invariably means that any performance conversations can be had without creating employee relations issues. Line managers who show a genuine interest in their team members and who are sensitive to the concerns of people on the frontline will create a better team culture and drive higher levels of performance. Line managers should understand their direct reports' motivations and should, as a minimum, be able to answer the following questions:

- What are their main career aspirations?

- What is their ideal job?

- What job would this person like to be doing two years from now, and why?

- What aspects of the job does this person most like and dislike?

- Name the three things most important to this person?

- Name three things that motivate or drive this person?

- What forms of recognition and awards does this person value most?

- What specific strengths does this person want to develop?

- What could you do to improve this person's working life?

- What specifically can demotivate this person?

- What hobbies and interests does this person have?

Line managers are responsible for setting organisational context, explaining how the work of each team member fits within this context and for keeping the team regularly appraised as to how they are doing. Their role is to coach their direct reports for performance in their current roles. Coaching is an essential component of a line manager's brief and should not be delegated. Why there is a whole coaching industry is a mystery to me. Why do organisations pay out vast sums of money to external consultants when this is simply the line manager's responsibility? Externals can be useful as a resource for missing pieces of an individual's overall jigsaw in terms of wisdom, skills or knowledge, but should not be engaged as performance coaches. Unfortunately, good coaching generally goes unrewarded and the lack of this skill is rarely penalised, which is an issue that organisations should be addressing.

Line managers are responsible for tasking their direct reports. This is simply a case of specifying what, by when, and with what resources (eg people, budget). Tasks should always be time-bound or they are just an ask. Where line managers are one work domain above their direct reports, sufficient discretionary space generally exists for these reports to be allowed to be trusted to get on with things.

Finally, line managers must be given enough authority to enable them to do their jobs and to enable them to be held accountable by their boss. Managers must:

• Be able to veto appointments to their teams.

• Be the people assigning tasks to their teams.

• Be able to make reward recommendations for their teams.

- Be able to initiate the removal of a direct report from their teams (whether the person should be exited from the organisation does not need to follow).

These responsibilities should not be delegated to or taken on by HR as this makes for impotent managers. People management, and specifically any 'hiring or firing', should be a function of the operational line as they know the business best.

Where a business operates from one location and trades Monday to Friday with no extended hours, there is no excuse for over-layering. This becomes much trickier in multi-site or extended trading scenarios, but every time you have a reporting relationship within the same work domain you will have compression and additional overhead cost, so try to avoid it wherever possible.

Within the operational domains it may be necessary to have team leaders as well as first-line managers or supervisors. The important point is that the team leaders are support roles not line roles, and should assist the manager with extended trading. They are there to operationally oversee their particular shift, but they do not become the de-facto frontline staff member's line manager. This is a subtle but important distinction.

Wherever possible I would try to avoid having expensive over-layering in the 'managing systems' domain. The regional management role in multi-site businesses is a substantial head of department role in complexity terms which is often not understood, nor appropriately remunerated. Regional managers reporting to divisional directors is a common set-up which creates significant tension and frustration and is felt across the operation. Where regional managers present as super-unit managers, a plan to upgrade the people in these roles would be the way forward rather than adding a compensatory layer.

Concept of the manager once-removed

Finally, I would like to introduce a concept which, when deployed, will transform your business. The fact that it is free makes it even more exciting. This is about clearly defining the role of the 'manager once-removed', or the 'skip manager'. The manager once-removed is an individual's manager's manager.

If the role of the line manager is to coach their direct reports for performance, the role of the manager once-removed is to focus firmly on development. The line manager covers 'how am I doing', while the manager once-removed covers 'what is my future'. This makes the manager once-removed the mentor. This philosophy firmly challenges the notion that individuals are randomly assigned a mentor. This process should absolutely be part of the line, and development of direct reports once-removed by the manager once-removed is an essential requirement of a management role. Do not allow this to be delegated or handed off.

Making talent management an essential function of the line at every level and firmly the responsibility of the manager once-removed is an important principle. Knowing direct reports once-removed means that when a vacancy arises, the manager once-removed is perfectly placed to know who to hire. In the absence of this framework, managers frequently ask their other direct reports who should fill the vacancy. This approach is flawed. The added advantage of cultivating trusted relationships with direct reports once-removed is that in the event there becomes an issue between a direct report once-removed and his or her manager, this is far more likely to be brought to the attention of the manager once-removed informally rather than in the form of a formal grievance.

I often get pushback on the basis that fulfilling the manager once-removed role in the way I prescribe is challenging because of the volume of people, but just one quality development conversation a year is sufficient when it is done well. In fact, these conversations are incredibly enjoyable because they are all about development. The impact on the individuals of their manager once-removed showing such interest should also not be underestimated. Where teams are small this is something that could perhaps occur over lunch, making it something even more special. There is no substitute for face-to-face conversations and the emotional engagement that results.

I recall one scenario I observed first-hand. A department manager who had been trained in the art of these development conversations took the time out to see a part-time staff member he felt had potential to become a manager. He sat with the individual for probably no more than thirty minutes, but the impact was incredible. Immediately the department manager left the store the part-time staff member rang her mum. 'Mum,' she said, 'you'll never guess what has just happened. My department manager has just come to the store, spent time with me and thinks I could be a manager.' The impact of the time spent with her solely focused on her development was amazing to observe in practise and it cost nothing other than the department manager's time. Everyone appreciates the opportunity of having an understanding manager sit down and discuss their career opportunities and to experience the positive effect of having their intuitive awareness of their own potential confirmed.

Differentiating between the performance conversations of a line manager and the development conversations of a manager once-removed is important. While a line manager may well have some development conversations, these should never replace those that are the responsibility of the manager once-removed. By contrast, a manager once-removed should never have performance conversations with a team member once-removed. This is very clearly the manager's job and to do so is to undermine the manager and confuses the team member.

7
Early Identification Of Changemakers

So far, we have outlined the right strategies to ensure a 'fit for purpose', culturally-aligned strategic and operational team. Now we can start to look forward at how to safeguard the business for tomorrow in leadership terms.

It is a statement of fact that organisations usually have everything they need in leadership pipeline terms. In the operational domains, they carelessly fail to recognise these individuals early enough. These individuals go off to fill another organisation's pipeline instead (these other organisations are often competitors) or they just set up their own businesses. In the strategic domains, high performing, long-serving executives are often mistakenly diagnosed as dinosaurs and overlooked in favour of external candidates, yet these internals are a known culture fit. They also have the benefit of deep organisational knowledge, experience and strong internal networks. Uniquely, as changemakers they have the thinking agility to reimagine all this knowledge and experience. These individuals have earlier been described as 'gold dust' and this point cannot be emphasised enough.

In terms of the science, future business leaders are those individuals on the steeper development curves. Rather than refer to these individuals as high potentials (which is usual), I refer to them as changemakers, and encourage leaders to do the same. The idea of 'high potential' somehow suggests that their value to the business is in the future rather than in the present, and that it serves as just a promotion label. The other question, of course, is potential for what?

The reality is that all changemakers immersed in the operational domains are incredibly valuable to leaders in the here and now, not just as a future pipeline of talent. They have the thinking agility to spot problems while at the same time are able to imagine new and innovative solutions. These are the individuals that leaders must seek out and spend time with.

The primary interpretation of the development curves is that 'the steeper the curve, the greater an individual's runway and career trajectory', but there is an interesting secondary twist that is incredibly valuable for talent spotting. This is the observation that the steeper development curve indicates an individual's greater speed of mental processing. So, when people make statements such as 'I really get that other person,' it is likely that each are on the same development curve and that it is the common speed of mental processing that is valued rather than any personality trait per se. This common speed of mental processing transcends age, so the best people to spot the changemakers are always the business leaders themselves – assuming of course that they have been confirmed as changemakers themselves as outlined in Chapter Four.

Changemakers will always spot and value other changemakers, whereas operators are unlikely to identify changemakers as talent because their frame of reference is more about time served and experience. The reality is that you identify with individuals on your own development curve, and as a result we each have our own talent bar and sense of what good looks like. Without education, it is unlikely that individuals would recognise someone on a steeper development curve than themselves as being more talented. They would see the person as different to themselves, but somehow this difference would not be processed or perceived positively. This presents some important considerations when setting up future business leader programmes and when considering who to put in charge of them.

There are three types of changemakers and the differences are important to note.

First are the changemakers who will ultimately do their best work as functional directors of national businesses or grow city-based or regional start-ups. They are the ones most commonly found and tend to be the only ones that stick around in large organisations. These individuals are identified by their capacity to serial process ('if/then' language) in their early to mid-twenties and parallel process ('if and only if' language) in their mid-thirties to early forties. They are able to keep up with the abstract thinking of the leaders but are able to convert it into a language that operators can understand. These changemakers make effective pivots between a leadership team and the frontline and are extremely valuable. They are generally highly sociable individuals who make obvious team leaders. Sociability is often disproportionately prized though, so this group is often overpromoted to CEO roles where they struggle with the increased complexity and under-hire, as we have already discussed.

Secondly, there are the rarer changemakers who will go on to make great CEOs of national businesses. These individuals are identified by their capacity to serial process on entry level and parallel process ('if and only if' language) early in their careers, ie by their late twenties and early thirties. The problem is that this group presents very differently. Their world is simple and different. They tend not to do small talk as this is seen as a waste of time and energy. In childhood this difference often kept them on the outside of things and not part of the popular gang. In large businesses their thinking agility is often overlooked because they are judged to lack sociability. They lack the need for sociability, so they often fail to realise that individuals in the operational domains require it. Generally speaking, where these individuals make it to CEO, their organisations should forgive their lack of 'small talk' in return for the vision and strategic direction they set which keep everyone successfully employed. In these scenarios, partner these individuals with a gregarious operations director or COO. PhD students regularly assess on this development curve and should be considered a valuable injection of future leadership talent alongside the more traditional MBA and graduate routes.

Finally, there are the very rare changemakers who could lead international and global businesses. These are true entrepreneurs who are unlikely to stick around in corporate life for long unless they are quickly identified. These individuals are identified by their capacity to parallel process ('if and only if' language) extremely early in their careers, in their mid-twenties. They tend to have the gregarious gene, but being so clever tend to require translators to be understood. Left to their own devices they will tend to recruit other very rare changemakers like themselves as they are naturally drawn to them. Where they can't find sufficient individuals on their wavelength, they will hire the next best thing – the rare changemakers. The problem here is that the more common and sociable changemakers who are the natural pivots are overlooked.

For the rare or very rare changemakers – those on the steepest development curves – their operational teams often complain about a group of clever people at the top that are out of touch with reality and who don't really seem to know what they are doing. Their lack of interest in site visits because of the abstract nature of their world means that this is often misinterpreted as a lack of interest or sensitivity by the frontline and perceived unfavourably as somewhat aloof and rude. Overlooking the emotional engagement of front-line teams and their need for absolute clarity over ambiguity is the risk for this group. An algorithm or application will never exist to replace people management. Another way to encourage and incentivise this group to get out and about in a business is to remind them that Fleming's discovery of penicillin, which changed the course of medicine, came about when his complexipacity lens enabled him to see more than dirty petri dishes. Newton similarly saw more than just a falling apple in discovering gravity.

An additional watch-out for leadership teams with high cognitive capability is that they often lack the experience or insight to appreciate the perspectives of loyal, hardworking, conscientious team members in the operational work domains or understand the conditions that they need to function effectively. For this reason, 'eyeball leadership' and a willingness to listen is important for this group. These problems tend not to occur with home-grown talent.

In the start-up arena the risk is that the entrepreneur and all his or her clever friends suffer with communication and translation issues.

The reality is that where the CEO, the functional directors and department heads are themselves changemakers, they become the organisation's most-effective chief talent officers. Where sourcing and identifying changemakers is delegated to talent managers, HR directors or external head-hunters, then be aware that without training they will usually only be able to spot and provide them if they are changemakers themselves.

Often the identification of changemakers falls out of the annual appraisal and succession planning cycle where the results are aggregated into some form of performance versus potential matrix. The problem with this is that while there is always hard data to support the placement of an individual in performance terms, the allocation of potential status is always much more subjective. Ask line managers and HR professionals on what basis they have allocated the potential status and there will be neither consistency nor rigour to any response. In the absence of a detailed knowledge of complexipacity the answers will always be highly subjective, and this subjectivity will be amplified when more line managers are involved. As a result, the wrong people are often put on a pedestal and training funds invested are erroneously allocated and wasted as a result. That this is often seen and ridiculed by the wider organisation is a bigger problem.

Use of assessment centres for identification should be avoided. Not only are they expensive to run, but by incorporating IQ and personality exercises the focus is put on the wrong things. Competency-based interviews should also be avoided, as this approach fails when looking to identify the potential to-do work which an individual is yet to experience. Put simply, they will be unable to answer questions in the 'tell me a time when' format. In the same way, external recruitment and online 'sifting' that eliminates candidates where they have no obvious prior experience will screen out changemakers every time.

As a good starting point, managers once-removed should ask individuals what they would like to achieve in their careers and over what timescales in their development discussions. It is possible to dig deeply and widely to identify changemakers by simply training line managers to spot the signs. In all cases the recommendations should always be validated with a complexipacity assessment.

If someone is going to do their best work in a strategic role then, by default, they will not do their absolute best work in the operational domains. They have to pass through these domains on their journey to get to there though. This is an important consideration, as these individuals are often held back from promotions because they are not 100% perfect and by doing this they go 'off the boil' through boredom and frustration and finally leave. A balance needs to be struck between performance and potential.

An interesting example springs to mind of a manager who was full of potential. Her reporting line was through an operationally focused leadership team. I was asked to assess four managers for suitability for a vacant managing systems domain role. I assessed all four candidates and suggested that only one of them would be able to handle the complexity of the vacant role. The trouble was that my recommendation was out of line with the judgement of the directors. The argument against the candidate I highlighted was that her standards were not the best. My view of the situation was that this manager was so badly out of flow, I was surprised she could summon the motivation to come to work each day. With some support my recommendation was approved. Six months later this individual was the one of the top performing managers. Within another six months she was recognised externally as the UK's most talented manager and that year's overall 'Rising Star'. Had it been down to her direct line managers though, her talent and potential would have been overlooked. It was a promotion the directors could never quite accept, and they would often comment on how much better the replacement manager for this person was. Of course the replacement was better, as she was better matched in complexipacity terms and as a consequence was much more in flow. The other consideration of course, is that this individual now posed a potential threat to their positions. This scenario plays out daily in business.

Later in the same organisation, a 'Future Business Leaders' programme was launched. Thirty internal individuals were nominated based on performance and perceived potential. Given that the line managers in charge of the nominations were all big enough for their own jobs, the likelihood was that these were good people. However, only seventeen were actually assessed, as a filtering process was imposed from the centre based on current performance. The problem with this blunt approach was that in some cases, these individuals had recently been moved and so the correlations being made were not absolute, or as they must have performed at some stage to be nominated, they had simply moved out of flow. Had we assessed them we may have been able to save them. Sadly, one year later all thirteen had left.

Another example demonstrates how easily changemakers can be hidden within the operational domains. An ex-colleague called me to ask what I thought of someone who had worked with us both on a turnaround assignment. I wasn't sure as I had never had any close dealings with the individual. On assessment, I was astounded to find this was undoubtedly a very rare changemaker who should certainly be hired by my ex-colleague – not least because he could be groomed to be his successor in time. What we both realised is that this individual had been quietly getting on with things, identifying problems and solving them without any need to escalate. So often it is the louder, less able but more showy colleagues keen to point out their problems and what they have done about them that get noticed. As a result, the more capable individuals who are just 'getting on with things' without any fuss can get overlooked because they make their work look easy.

Changemaker characteristics

Let us look at the clues that might suggest an individual is a changemaker and future business leader. As a minimum, I would encourage leadership teams to train the operational teams in these 'signs' and try to create a development culture whereby operators are rewarded for talent spotting and for sponsoring these individuals.

In the first instance, always show an interest in what an individual is doing outside of work. In the scenario that individuals are not being fully challenged at work, they will often be using their spare capacity outside of the workplace. I recall an assistant manager, described as a nightmare by his manager. Alerted to the potential 'troublemaker' label, I spent some time with the individual. Outside of work, he was running a global web business. On assessment, he ultimately had potential to be a CEO of an international business. Unfortunately, this was not an organisation where potential was nurtured. The individual left and a future potential CEO talent was unnecessarily lost.

I actually think of my own father's career choices differently now. He was a schoolteacher and chose to teach in one of the roughest and most deprived schools in Leeds, which at the time I never understood. Alongside this, he ran Yorkshire Schools Cricket on a voluntary basis, which consumed most evenings, weekends and every summer holiday. I see clearly now that this is how he found his own sense of 'flow'.

Getting a sense of how much complexity an individual is exposing themselves to is another clue. Interviewing an Italian deputy manager for a promotion, I enquired as to why she had decided to come to England. She spoke six languages and her decision to come to England was based on the fact that English was her worst language. If we think about this scenario, most people would go to the country where their language skills were the most proficient. In effect she was exposing herself to the greatest level of complexity. Along the same lines, a junior designer I met recently successfully completed his degree with a 2:1. On further investigation, the candidate was from a small village in Tenerife and a poor background. He had come to England because there was no student loan facility in Spain. To cover his living costs, he worked twenty-four hours a week in a hotel. So, his 2:1 against all of the background of difficulty would be comparable to someone with a First studied in their mother tongue and with better economic parental support and no need to work to supplement their income.

Finally, I think about an early interaction with a store manager in a new role. Driving to make a few store visits he talked me through his career history, explaining that he had started his career as a teacher on the basis that he would be able to add real value, derive some worthwhile purpose and ultimately change the world. His experience was of a profession steeped in bureaucracy and he soon realised teaching was not what he had thought it to be. While chatting, I pulled out a leaflet from his glove compartment. This was his own 'Zorbing' business which he ran on the side with his partner. Given he lived near Cambridge, his biggest money-earning opportunity was around the time of the university 'May Balls'. I quickly clocked that this was an individual capable of more and lobbied for him to receive an early promotion despite the CEO of this business valuing experience and time served over top talent. As a regional manager he went on to be the organisation's highest performer, consistently over-achieving on his targets.

Other things to consider and to educate operational management to look out for are individuals that display the following characteristics:

- Question the existing rules and assumptions and experiment with different approaches. Wary of 'establishment thinking'.

- Grow out of their roles more quickly than average.

- Get bored quickly once they know how to do something.

- Look for second and third order consequences and unexpected developments given an ability to see further down the line.

- Show interest in external influences, eg markets, investors, competitors, suppliers and technology developments.

- Have a need to understand the 'why' as well as the 'what' and 'how'.

- Quick learners, eg seeing implications and sensitivities faster than usual and understanding the bigger picture beyond the immediate task.

- Work out 'the rules of the game' or the 'unwritten rules' even if they are buried in distracting detail.

- See ambiguity as providing space for change and creativity. A tendency to be excited rather than fazed by uncertainty.

- Classed as poor listeners when in fact they just 'get it' quickly, don't need to hear more and just want to move on.

- Are able to plan, even in times of turbulence. In a crisis they tend to rise to the fore.

- Build empires to access more complex work to find their own sense of flow. This causes tensions as boundaries are crossed with their boss and their peers.

Where there are differences in output this is usually related to greater complexipacity rather than hard work. Those with more capability will appear less busy or rushed as they are mentally managing more data, working in a more organised way and doing less by trial and error, and yet it is often those seen to be working the hardest and the longest hours that are valued more.

No organisation can hope to gain a competitive advantage unless it can identify, develop and champion changemakers. The talent pool also needs to be full and not just occupied by a small number of crown princes/princesses. Identification is one thing, but it is the development these individuals are then provided with, and over what accelerated timeframes, that will determine whether this potential is ultimately converted.

Identification of changemakers is also vital for smaller nations. They should be considered as a scarce national resource and identified, retained and repatriated wherever possible. I reflect on New Zealand, where I have had many years of experience both as a tourist and as a contributor to their vibrant start-up community. The problem starts with the overseas experience that so many students take after education. Overseas travel adds complexity and uncertainty and therefore appeals more readily to changemakers than operators. As a result, a large percentage of this already scarce resource disappears immediately, with no guarantee that it will return. For those that do return, they often leave again when they outgrow the roles and the salaries available locally. If they could be encouraged and incentivised to return/remain in New Zealand, they could grow these smaller companies into international and global organisations.

Uneducated changemakers are another pool of overlooked talent. Their spare complexipacity will be going somewhere though. These are individuals who are probably doing great things for their communities on a voluntary basis. At the other extreme, these are often gang leaders, drug barons and the like. In both examples, their significant cognitive capacity cannot be used for legitimate, paid economic work due to their lack of education. Finding ways to convert the latter group would certainly provide a new angle when rehabilitating offenders.

8
Championing Changemakers

When it comes to the development of change-makers, the ultimate responsibility and ownership for this must sit firmly with the CEO and the leadership team, ensuring no boundaries or blockages to movement. Leadership development needs to be part of the overall business strategy such that it is embedded in an organisation's culture and seen as an investment, not a cost that disappears when the going gets tough. For changemakers, finding these organisations represents the ultimate perk. Delegating the development of future business leaders to HR and the training team will just not work, especially in the event that the HR and training team are not change-makers themselves.

A culture of internal promotion ahead of external recruitment can only be successfully achieved where there is leadership team sponsorship, and where this exists it will always be a source of competitive advantage. Changemakers will always favour and look to join an organisation that can demonstrate – with evidence rather than just words – their commitment and support to an 'internals first, externals by exception' approach. Organisations that rely on external hires where internal individuals already have the proven skills and experience will haemorrhage their changemakers and fail to attract new ones. This is because for the external who has already done it before, it is a job but not a promotion. External recruitment based on prior skills and knowledge is often favoured over internal promotion as it is perceived to present less risk, but without a complexipacity assessment and a robust check against a cultural framework the reality is that it is far more risky on every level.

The head-hunting model is generally based on the risk-adverse approach of ensuring that individuals have already done everything previously so organisations placing a heavy emphasis on external hires through head-hunters are likely to be missing out on the best talent, and most certainly missing out on leadership potential. In any event, prior experience and skills are becoming less and less relevant in a world of increased volatility, uncertainty, complexity and ambiguity. The case for the development of changemakers, with their ability to reinvent prior experiences in the light of new contexts, has never been stronger and is the way forward. Young changemakers are now looking towards the start-up arena given the perception that they represent better learning cultures, so the competition for talent in the corporate arena is a very real one.

As we talked about identifying changemakers early we need to also prioritise their development early. Unless both of these aspects are addressed simultaneously, the result will be the turnover of this group. All too often organisations have a 'one size fits all' development proposition where a set number of rotations have to occur over an agreed timeline. I particularly recall assessing a candidate for a promotion who had initially been excluded from a development programme by her line manager on the basis that she had not fulfilled the criteria of having been a manager for a minimum of two years. She was an exceptional talent and had she not challenged the rules I am sure she would have ended up even more bored than she was already and a definite leaver.

Whenever I spend time with changemakers, what they crave is the opportunity to work on real business issues with real business data and real consequence, ie on the job. I would encourage the creation of a cohort (or cohorts) of changemakers from across the business and from across the various work domains which the CEO and leadership team can effectively use as an internal entrepreneurial change consultancy. They can tackle current and future business issues, giving them great networking exposure to the leadership team, great exposure to wider business issues, and invaluable credibility. In addition, where leadership teams have new thinking, these individuals will be able to give an operational perspective on how to take the new thinking forward. The danger of presenting new thinking to operators is that they often don't see these new ideas as good ideas and more than often dismiss them out of hand due to an inability to mentally construct anything that doesn't already exist. They think they are acting in the organisation's best interests, when in fact a great piece of strategic thinking has just been missed.

Where any classroom activity takes place, what will be important is the mental processing capacity of the classroom trainer. Unless they are a changemaker themselves and operating in a more complex work domain than the delegates, they will fail to inspire. The leadership development curriculum should be firmly rooted in work domain transitions.

The completion of a complexipacity assessment on all changemakers allows us to pace careers with a great deal of certainty. Given that cognitive potential grows with age and at a predictive rate, once we know where an individual is today we can extrapolate this out to pace their future journey and give robust guidance on when individuals will be ready to transition from one domain of work complexity to another.

For this group, it is important to think of their development as less of a race and more of a journey. Organisations must not be tempted to move unprepared changemakers into strategic roles too soon, as these are substantial, business-critical roles. Many failed leaders would have gone on to be successful if the organisation and / or the individual had been more patient. The best development for young changemakers is to get them into a substantial department head role at the earliest opportunity and use this domain for lateral functional moves and experimentation. Where businesses are international, this is a great time to expose them to different cultural experiences. Turnaround and start-up opportunities at this level are also exciting considerations. Ensure though that they don't 'butterfly' through assignments and that they spend sufficient time on each assignment to fix problems properly.

The best leaders invariably spend considerable time in substantial department head roles and have ideally held operational roles as well as specialist roles. The benefit is that they gain a deeper understanding of the departments they have worked in, and as a result when they take on a more complex role they are not fazed when presented with business or people problems. Directors with strong operational management experience are never afraid to exit an underperforming direct report because, in the worst-case scenario, they know they can always cover the role temporarily themselves while a replacement is found without worrying that things will fall apart. By contrast, directors without this depth of experience often tolerate underperforming direct reports for fear of what would happen if they were left with a gap. This phenomenon is most apparent with ex-strategy consultants who often find themselves employed by a business by virtue of some excellent consultancy work, but they lack the experience of leading and motivating large operational teams. Despite all the advances in technology, as already stated, there will never be an algorithm or application written to replace people management and therefore future leaders need to learn these skills as early in their careers as possible.

Positioning changemakers

I am often asked if anything can be done to accelerate an individual's development. The 'seeds' of their ultimate potential are always there, and these are what generate the notion of 'flair', but these seeds can't be fully relied on before they mature. This is why you will often get these flashes of genius from among a greater number of totally unworkable suggestions, and sometimes the sense that changemakers might believe that they are better than they are. The world isn't an exact science though, so there may be times where an individual is given a role slightly early. What is important in these instances is that the person promoted is supported with strategic decision making and resourcing decisions to ensure no under-hiring occurs. The business must also clearly identify who is accountable for providing this support.

In multi-site organisations I would recommend moving changemakers identified in the field into the corporate centre as soon as possible, and ideally into departments of key strategic importance. Often businesses find themselves taking people into the centre on the basis of time served, in that somehow 'it's their turn' with their experience and length of service being the primary triggers. The problem is that usually these individuals are operators who don't have the thinking agility to create anything 'new' from these prior experiences. In addition, operators in an HQ environment tend to keep their heads below the parapet. The combination of both of these factors means that the operational voice which was intended from the move is rarely heard and ex-colleagues are left feeling that these individuals have somehow 'forgotten their roots'. By contrast, changemakers have the thinking agility to make their prior experience count and usually have a head that stays well above the parapet to ensure they are heard.

Be aggressive when changemakers are identified in the specialist functions. They will always benefit from a substantial line management role. Managing one or two specialists as commented on earlier is not management. A management role is only such if 50% of time is actively spent on management. In addition, the management of large numbers of frontline resource generally brings with it far more day-to-day challenges given extended trading, seven-day working and the general problems encountered by individuals struggling on lower incomes.

The benefit of experimenting in the managing systems domain is that generally mistakes are easier to tolerate. Leadership teams should pay attention culturally to how they handle mistakes. Learning from mistakes is a powerful development tool. An organisation that doesn't tolerate mistakes won't have anyone admitting to them or learning from them. By contrast, a more developmentally focused organisation will look at how the person handled things and what was learned.

I recall a particular organisation with a CEO who was to changemakers what the child-catcher in *Chitty Chitty Bang Bang* was to children, believing them to be 'smart arses' who needed bringing down a peg or two. While the public humiliation dished out routinely and publicly was invariably character-building and an experience to reflect on after the event, what this demonstrates is that a development culture can't be created from halfway down an organisation. A 'fit for purpose' leadership team constituted as outlined in Chapter Four will always create a development culture that enables talent to thrive. In the event that there are cultural issues, then an organisation needs to circle back to the leadership team, address the issues and repeat the previous chapters.

I would like to return to the concept of the 'manager once-removed' at this point. This is the mentoring role, and where this is done properly and objectively it should create trusted relationships that make internal development extremely high profile while also quickly spotting where there could be issues with line managers.

A common issue easily identified by the manager once-removed is the scenario where the line manager is taking the credit for the work of their direct report. I recall a junior marketeer who had lots of previous experience. Yet the line manager kept referring to her as an 'administrator'. The reality of the situation was that the subordinate, a very rare changemaker, was doing all the hard work and the line manager was taking all the glory (think of a modern-day Cinderella). Fortunately, the owner had been made aware of the manager once-removed principles and, having put them to the test, quickly found out what was going on. The business retained a potential future director and CEO of the business and the manager was exited.

Another point worth recapping is the paradox that if someone is going to do their best work in a leadership role then by default, they will not do their absolute best work in the earlier domains although they still have to pass through these on their journey to the level where they will. An optimal balance needs to be struck, because holding them back until they are perfect won't work. Often those lobbying for perfection are those that have already reached their level and so perfection is achievable for them.

Sponsoring this group has great benefit for organisations that are in change, in turnaround or that are facing an uncertain future – not least because changemakers thrive on the uncertainty and are usually highly resilient and resourceful. I recall an organisation which had new owners and a new business model looming. As a result of this many were leaving and given the lack of certainty about the future it would have been disingenuous to try to stop them where they had secured a more stable role. In restructuring, rather than recruit interims, fixed-term contractors or agency temps, we deliberately embarked on a strategy to fill every leadership role by promoting an internal changemaker wherever they existed. The individuals that were promoted were thrilled. Adding value to their CVs and wanting to have their new role on their CVs for as long as possible, they stuck with us. One particular hire really stuck out as head of E-commerce. There were calls from the CEO to go with an experienced, proven, external contractor who would have been extremely expensive. Instead the director and I, who had been exposed to complexipacity previously, opted to back a twenty-six-year-old junior E-commerce manager who we also established actually had some good commercial experience from a previous organisation. With some great support from his experienced and wise boss he was a sensation. That opportunity helped him to secure a great next role when things finally wound up. When I last checked he was in San Francisco on an international assignment heading up a global team.

What the above example demonstrates is that risks can be taken on young talent who are not completely qualified as long as you can fill in the missing gaps in the individual's personal jigsaw somehow. In the above example, the individual had sufficient mental processing capacity, was a great culture fit, had the motivation and drive to take on the promotion but lacked experience. All it needed was for his boss to provide a little bit of extra support and occasionally some wise counselling when coaching him. Where the gap is a specific skill or piece of knowledge and this cannot be sourced internally, identifying experienced externals is the trick. There are lots of experienced, knowledgeable, wise and emotionally mature individuals out there who would be happy to be available to help for a couple of hours a week. This is a much more cost-effective proposition than an expensive external hire and the inevitable cost of turnover of the overlooked internal. The external is only engaged to train in a specific piece of skilled knowledge though. They are not engaged as a performance coach, as this is the role of the line manager and this role should never be delegated.

Where organisations really do get behind their internal talent the result is a rewarding win-win on both counts. Both start-ups and corporates could benefit from developing the concept of focusing on potential and figuring out how to develop the skills and experience. Extraordinary competitive advantage would follow. What is the alternative to identifying promising talent and nurturing it? An external-only strategy cannot and should not win in any event.

Yet this whole arena is such a visible one. Being seen to sponsor the wrong people can be toxic and damaging for both the leadership team and the individuals. Organisations need to be certain that this group is monitored regularly to ensure that they continue to perform and continue to demonstrate behaviours in line with the organisation's culture and values. Being part of a future leadership cohort should be seen and positioned as a privilege and not a guaranteed right, and deselection from the group should always be a consideration.

Developing necessary skills

Optimal communication occurs between individuals who are in the same work domain and also on the same development curve as they view the world through the same lens. The difficulty comes when you have differences. I come across so many changemakers who think they are going crazy because they don't understand why others don't see what they do. The simple fact is they don't, and once this is understood a huge weight is usually lifted.

Where changemakers are managing operational teams there can be a great deal of difference. We tend to communicate at our own level, and because we understand what we are saying we therefore assume that others understand too. It is always the change-maker's responsibility to communicate a message at a level that can be understood by others, not the reverse, and to actively cultivate a culture whereby their teams are encouraged to speak up when they don't understand without fear of being considered in any way stupid. Learning social skills and the importance of small talk is a must and it is for this reason that the big department head operational roles are such great development experiences.

I recall a serious example of communication problems when a failed sales campaign resulted in a £1 million hit to the bottom line and a profits warning for a major PLC. In this example, the sales director in question was capable and genuinely believed they had correctly interpreted the CEO's instructions.

Leadership requires great listening skills rather than doing all the talking. This requires patience and empathy and listening for what is being said as well as for what isn't being said, or what is being avoided. It is quite OK for the leadership team not to know everything and so it is wise to develop humility in changemakers early, which can also help to avoid the 'smart arse, know it all' labels that are often applied to them in their early careers. Dismissing ideas of direct reports and team members can be avoided by listening and by using the 'show me' concept, which immediately triggers a concrete discussion. Listening is also a great way to build and engender strong networks with teams, bosses, peers, suppliers and customers. Networking at every level is an important skill not to be reserved just for leadership teams. Building diverse, strong internal networks and relationships is vital for this group and its importance should be drummed in early.

Finally, having an accurate view of oneself is another protection against derailing. This requires the ability to ask for, and positively accept, feedback from an early stage. Rather than expensive and bureaucratic 360 written or computer-driven feedback mechanisms, I would always encourage face-to-face dialogue. I have found the most successful way of achieving this is to encourage changemakers to regularly seek out two or three aspects of behaviour that their peers, direct reports and bosses admire, as well as one or two aspects of behaviour that they would like to be worked on. Another angle on this is to ask for feedback on what the changemaker should be doing more of (or conversely, what they should be doing less of).

There is a lot of current debate on boardroom quotas and diversity. Even once identified as potential future leaders, this diverse group often still lack confidence and belief. Additional focus, encouragement and strong mentoring is therefore recommended, particularly given that all the evidence suggests that greater diversity on leadership teams drives greater profits.

The best development culture in the world, however, will be immediately undermined if the final piece of The Changemaker Effect is not attended to, that of 'Reward'.

9
Reward And The Importance Of Equity

The sobering fact is that if we fail on reward, the 'disproportionate angst' experienced by the organisation will be enormous and insurmountable in both engagement and labour turnover terms. Pay is a serious and emotional issue.

Individuals have a reasonably accurate sense of fairness where 'weight' of role is concerned, and any perceived inequity is more toxic and explosive than anything else. Forget external equity – lack of internal equity is the worst and most insidious of crimes. It is all about differentials and these differentials are usually widely felt and discussed. Organisations that believe otherwise are sadly misguided. A performance culture can only genuinely follow where people's contributions are both recognised and fairly rewarded.

Despite an organisation's considerable commitments in this area, which may include investments in in-house reward experts, expensive reward consultants and even more expensive job evaluation systems, employee engagement surveys continue to highlight problems with pay and the perceived absence of a fair deal. Given that the gap between executive and front-line pay continues to increase, this perceived inequity is getting worse, and if the gap is too large it creates a sense of defeat as individuals feel both unimportant and exploited. Add to this the current problems with the gender pay gap and it is clear that current systems are not working.

Job evaluation is by its very definition an opinion, a judgement and in many cases pure guesswork. It is not an absolute measurement and where there is disagreement there is no absolute yardstick for reso-lution, generally just more debate. It is often decision making by committee and smart people can generally manipulate it. What evaluation systems consistently fail to take account of is the inherent complexity of a role. This is determined neither by the number of direct reports nor by the size of an individual's budget, and yet these are the factors that form the typical corner-stones of most available methodologies. Additionally, and critically, the system for determining reward is never the same system that is then used for selection. In the same way, salary surveys are just a comparison of roles with the same job titles which may or may not have the same complexity requirements.

The real consideration of a successful reward strategy requires an understanding of both the complexity of the role and the complexipacity of the person either already in the role or the person being considered for the role. Size of role versus size of person is the key. Individuals naturally seek employment and a salary at a level commensurate with their complexipacity and so the issue is often not that the individual is underpaid, but rather that they are underemployed.

Let us take the millennial debate as a current case in point. There is so much critical debate around about the inappropriate demands made by this group of individuals. These are individuals who have been encouraged to rack up student debt to get a university degree, which generally requires an individual to have complexipacity in the 'judgement outside routine' domain. Yet when these individuals enter the workplace, they often take on 'judgement within routine' work and often on the minimum wage. The reality is that they are capable of handling work with more complexity and their perceived 'unreasonable demands' are merely a cry for work with more complexity which would come with the additional reward. It is not a pay issue at all but rather an opportunity issue. The greater the long-term potential of the new job entrant, the wider the discrepancy between the frontline role and what he or she is really capable of. Where an individual is underemployed and underpaid, life is doubly unrewarding and labour turnover is practically guaranteed.

This is hardly a new problem. I recall my own entry into the workplace where I had the luxury of a twelve-month graduate development programme delivered at significant cost. After all that investment, our first roles out of training were not complex enough and within two years all the changemakers had left. This model and churn continued to repeat for years with no diagnosis of the real underlying issue.

Domain of work is the common measurement that allows us to link the complexity of the work, the complexipacity of the person and fair pay.

As we have stated previously, a complexipacity assessment is the only robust way to establish what work an individual is capable of, which in turn drives their associated reward expectations. In its absence, a data point we can consider is the issue of time – and the time that we are talking about is the 'time horizon afforded for discretion'. I am not by any means saying that time horizon is the most important thing about a job, but it can be used as an absolute and objective measure of its complexity requirement.

With the allocation of any task there will always be a prescribed and a discretionary element. The prescribed limits are defined standards which are always clear, specific, concrete and need no further interpretation, eg visit large customers once a month, complete a certain number of calls per day. The jobholder needs to use his or her discretion and judgement to determine how to organise the work and to determine the appropriate pace to apply to the work. It is this exercise of discretion over a given timeframe that determines the weight of a job, and the greater the complexity of a role, the longer the timelines of discretionary effort that the jobholder will be allowed.

The task in the role that has the longest target completion time will determine the weight and work level of the role, while the longer the timeframes for successfully applying discretionary effort, the more complexity an individual can handle. It is often necessary to reassure individuals that we are not looking to assess or judge the speed with which the task has been completed to stop them artificially shortening the timeframes of any assignment.

The person who has the best awareness of this measurement is the line manager. Large numbers of reward and HR professionals are not necessary where line managers are fully trained and empowered to make these assessments. In the event of a disagreement then the line manager's manager (the 'manager once-removed') becomes the arbitrator.

In the absence of the assessment, when trying to gauge the potential work level of an individual, when delegating a task the manager has to decide how long in timeframe terms he or she would be confident to give the person in order for the task to be successfully completed. In other words, would the manager give the individual a three-month task to work on, or would he or she decide that the task needed to be broken down into three discrete one-month chunks, with one chunk to be completed and assessed before starting the next?

Calculating equity fairly

In Chapter Four we outlined what to consider when configuring a team and highlighted some of the top line 'watch outs' which might suggest there are problems. A mismatch in capability in leadership roles is the single biggest inhibitor to a company's growth and leads to individuals being overpaid for the work they can really handle. Individuals always have a sense of this, so it leads to neuroticism, insecurity and stress. Deep down, they know they are earning more than they deserve and that the organisation could find someone better and they tend to take their paranoia out on their direct reports because they know that they know it too.

The sense of a lack of internal equity is felt most in work domains closest to the frontline though, where there can be a considerable mismatch between the complexity of a role and what the jobholder can actually handle, as outlined in the case of the millennial debate. Addressing this waste of talent in the first instance would go a long way to resolving pay issues. Looking at reward in this way puts internal development and equality of opportunity at the centre of an organisation's reward strategy. Looking at the gender pay gap as more of an opportunity gap for undiagnosed or unsupported changemaking females, for example, would be far more useful and valuable.

Beyond the mismatching of role and person, the discretion afforded to frontline jobs can also be very different from one company to another, even if the job title is the same. There is a great deal of difference between frontline roles where most of the work is prescribed and where problems outside of any prescribed limits requires escalation to a supervisor when compared to roles where judgement is encouraged, yet often the salaries offered are the same. By default, the minimum wage covers the roles of least complexity so where more judgement is required the minimum wage becomes inappropriate.

Paying staff more than the minimum wage on the face of it always looks like an additional cost for a business, but an analysis of the real cost of labour turnover including all the hidden costs will generally create the business case. I encourage all CEOs to convert labour turnover percentages into hard cash so that the impact of churn is more tangible and concrete. There are many models available and the costs are anything from one year of salary to five years of salary depending on the role and the location. The numbers are always horrifying when presented in this way.

In businesses where relationships are important, labour turnover and even more importantly, stability of staff become key metrics. I particularly recall my time at a 'rent to own' business where any movement of staff resulted in higher levels of debt. This was because the customers were not paying the business, they were paying the people that they knew. If the people changed, the relationship broke down and the customers didn't pay. Given it was a business based on personal relationships, we had to minimise movement and labour turnover. The frontline work was not minimum wage work, as often the results of the judgements made by the frontline would not be seen for three months. There were two reasons for the turnover: for those who could handle the complexity the reward was insufficient, and for those hired in with a complexipacity aligned to minimum wage work the job was too much for them. By laying out the real content of the job and paying an appropriate salary for it, both labour turnover and the debt reduced. The business case for improving pay was more than covered.

Another organisation had the opposite problem. They actually paid good money for their entry level roles and were proud of the high percentage of graduates that applied as a result. To successfully achieve a degree, as previously stated in the millennial debate, usually requires a capability with discretionary timeframes of three months or more. In this organisation the new hires were attracted by the salary, only to find the complexity of the work woefully lacking, resulting in high levels of turnover despite the good starting salary. This was resolved by separating out the 'judgement within routine' work and hiring individuals well-matched to it. In this organisation, salary costs came down because in the original model they were overpaying for the work. This demonstrates that for true engagement, the salary and the level of complexity of the work have to be matched.

In the same organisation, we noticed that management churn was high. On closer analysis, and having completed some assessments, this almost always coincided with the store managers transitioning in complexipacity between 'judgement outside routine' work and 'managing systems' work. With only a small number of field management roles available when compared to the number of store managers, we either needed to relook at the model or accept the store management churn, but this was a relationship business and fortunately the organisation had a CEO who really grasped the significance of complexity. We needed to find a way to increase the complexity of the store manager role while also being prepared to increase pay accordingly. What we decided was to create a model whereby stores and the store manager would have more autonomy and freedom than had previously been the case. We described a 'franchise-lite' model whereby the store managers would have control of their inventory and budget and gain a share of their stores profits thereby increasing their overall compensation. As a result, less span breaking field managers were required as they were now able to manage by exception, salaries balanced out overall and a more empowered culture developed.

This example illustrates the problems in most multi-site retail and hospitality employment models. Where unit manager roles are set and remunerated in the 'judgement outside routine' domain, command and control cultures follow. This leads to low employee engagement, high churn rates and unnecessary and expensive layers of bureaucracy by way of compensation.

In many organisations broad-banding has been adopted and often these broad bands overlap. Looking through the lens of complexipacity challenges the idea of overlapping bands. If an individual has outgrown the complexity of a role, they need to be found a new one, or alternatively, ways to add more complexity to the current role need to be found in the short term. Overpaying for a role or individual will not be sustainable long term: the individual will ultimately be unable to find 'flow' in this scenario and either boredom, dissatisfaction or both will kick in.

Incentives and bonuses

It is quite common to find leaders to be rather out of touch with the challenges of making ends meet on the frontline. As a consequence, they are often relatively naïve when it comes to understanding the lengths the frontline will go to in order to manipulate incentives if it means they can earn more as a result. The result is that incentives often do not achieve what they set out to and business is somehow damaged. Where incentives are poorly thought out, they can often act as a disincentive and ironically create more angst than had the incentive not existed in the first place.

An amusing story to demonstrate this springs to mind. My CEO asked me to create a new 'Red Letter Day' styled incentive for the frontline. I worked on it diligently and was excited when the time came to present it but it quickly became clear that what I had understood as an additional incentive to complement the existing cash incentive was not his understanding. He wanted to replace the existing cash incentive with the non-cash incentive. When I explained that the frontline staff used their bonuses to pay their mortgages, he seemed genuinely shocked. Wherever possible, I advocate paying salaries that match the complexities of the work and having bonuses that are exactly that.

One issue with bonuses arises when they are linked to group performance over and above individual performance. This is fine where the salary for the role is well-matched to the role in complexity terms because then the bonus is exactly as it should be. Where a management bonus is relied on to compensate for an inadequate salary though, there will be problems where achievement of that bonus is outside of the individual's total control.

In the world of start-ups and entrepreneurs there is the same problem when it comes to equity. Using it to compensate for poor base salaries is not sustainable. For the entrepreneur, the risk is there by default, but where individuals are employed factoring in the equity piece can be dangerous as it can be neither guaranteed nor relied upon.

Where businesses are underperforming the frontline should not be penalised. The responsibility for the underperformance sits with the CEO and the leadership team. Where frontline staff are underperforming then remove them, but those that are performing should be paid a salary appropriately aligned to the complexity of their roles.

Where individuals are using spare capability outside of work on an unpaid basis consideration should be given to see whether more complex work can be found so that the individual can benefit financially from their additional capacity. Voluntary work should not be used to compensate for the lack of economic work.

In many businesses, individual contributors are forced to become managers to improve their remuneration. This way of thinking is seriously flawed for two reasons. Firstly, managers of individual contributors are not managers as they do not spend at least half of their time managing, and secondly, by calling them a manager they then mistakenly believe, or are encouraged to believe, they should delegate work. As a result, specialist work is often delegated to too low a level and competitive advantage is lost. Significantly complex work can exist in the specialist functions and where this is encouraged it will always represent competitive advantage, particularly where a key role is placed in a domain more complex than that of a competitor and the jobholder is well-matched.

While salaries will vary within domains according to the different associated timeframes, what should remain consistent are the benefits. Allocating benefits packages by work domain really does make things extremely straightforward.

When it comes to changemakers and reward, there are major considerations and it is for these reasons that they need to be the responsibility of the leadership team. Given the pace with which they move through the work domains, standard annual increases will never be sufficient to match salary with complexipacity and it may not be in the individual's or the company's interests to move their job roles each year. Also, as previously stated, where changemakers butterfly their way around an organisation they will usually fail – from a business perspective they never stay anywhere long enough for their performance to be truly evaluated, and on a personal level they never put in the 'hard yards' in any role for long enough to really learn from the experience.

Given that generally people have a reasonably accurate and intuitive sense of fairness where 'weight' of role is concerned, one thing to consider when faced with matters of pay inequality is to ask the individual what he or she thinks would be fair. Try it. I promise that you will generally be surprised by the responses you receive. Often, what is considered to be fair is not that much of a difference, yet it is driving considerably disproportionate angst. In the cases of any pay challenge, complexipacity assessments are always recommended as they provide all the answers required to make a fair decision. As discussed, just because people have the same job title and the same standard job description it does not always guarantee that they are doing the same work.

As a general rule of thumb consider that total remuneration should increase by a factor of two by each work domain. The minimum wage of a country gives you the base line and starting point. Separating out cost of living increases from increases for added work complexity increases is the key. If the minimum wage rises by 2% annually, make this a generic cost of living increase to maintain the appropriate work domain differentials. Over and above this, increase salaries only when there is an increase in work complexity and increase it in the moment at the point of the change. At the strategic domains, an optimal balance between fixed and variable pay allows for bonuses to be entre-preneurially earned. This approach would save all the work and all the frustrations of the annual appraisal and pay review ritual which most detest.

Finally, there is much debate about pay differentials and whether sufficient payment is going to frontline workers. Working this equation in reverse, starting with the CEO salary and dividing by a factor of two by each work level would drive out some interesting relative total compensation payments for frontline workers in some organisations. The calculation certainly acts as a good check and balance on relative fairness.

10
Are You Ready?

Failing to assemble the right leadership team quickly is the number one reason businesses fail. Successful CEOs always focus on people and culture ahead of product or technology.

Backing the wrong players from the off will waste at least eighteen months of valuable time with serious consequences for the leaders themselves, for the organisations they are entrusted to lead and for the people who rely on the organisation's success for work.

In general, the people piece is not working, and this was exemplified recently when speaking with a FTSE 250 company. By their own admission, they were fully aware of the 'Peter Principle' because they were always doing it, they had forty people on a leadership programme (of whom over half in their opinion were the wrong people) and, finally, their policy was to only recruit externally at a senior level. Despite all of this, they did not feel they needed any help. If this is occurring in a FTSE company, with all the resources it has available to it, then what can be certain is that to a greater or lesser extent the same issues are playing out across corporations, small- and medium-enterprises and start-ups across the globe.

When it comes to people, what is lacking is an overall system that has rigour and is joined up across selection, promotion, training and development, organisation design and reward. The Changemaker Effect is a scientifically proven model and when its steps are followed it will transform organisations by creating well-structured and well-led teams, leading to a culture of innovation and creativity. In turn, this allows internal talent across the spectrum of diversity to thrive while, ironically, driving down costs at the same time.

At the heart of The Changemaker Effect are two key statements:

People management is done best 'in the line': Coaching, mentoring and talent spotting responsibilities are anchored firmly in the roles of the manager and manager once-removed respectively. This eliminates the need for expensive external coaches and mentors and drives out a requirement for much smaller and more strategically focused HR teams. Training in the principles is all that is required, and a highly motivated, empowered and effective line is the result.

Internal talent is best: Most organisations have all the talent they need but lack overall understanding and the methodology to hunt it out. The latter is particularly the case in the operational domains. Identifying and mobilising underutilised talent while simultaneously realigning overstretched talent is the trick.

Internals are a known culture fit and already have the networks to work at pace. To create The Changemaker Effect requires complexipacity and culture fit to drive hiring decisions, filling skills and experience gaps with targeted short-term internal or external support. This is in direct contrast to buying in the skills and experience of failed externals who continue to be recycled in an environment where referencing is highly manipulative.

The Changemaker Effect

To recap on the steps that are required and the order in which they need to be addressed:

- Organisation Design (Chapter 2)
  - Structure follows strategy and is always the first step in the model.

- - Only add layers where they contribute value so that talent can thrive, and payroll overhead can be optimised.

- Leadership Team (Chapter 4)

  - - The capability of the CEO and the leadership team is the single biggest predictor of future business and investment performance.

  - - In the case of a CEO or chairman, the best time to complete this human capital due diligence is between acceptance of a role and commencement.

  - - In the case of M&A and investment decisions, it should be done alongside the financial due diligence.

- Culture (Chapter 5)

  - - A strong culture is a strategic enabler and the capability of the leadership team has the biggest impact on this.

  - - Where poor performance is not explained by complexipacity, poor cultural fit will be the answer. Building a robust framework allows this to be easily highlighted and swiftly addressed.

- Talent (Chapter 6)

  - - Everyone is talented when correctly matched to their role and where they are a culture fit.

- Looking at talent through the lens of complexipacity eliminates all gender, age, ethnic, educational, culture and unconscious biases, making it the ultimate diversity tool.

• Identifying Changemakers (Chapter 7)

- Organisations, institutions and nations need to look deep and wide both internally and externally and assume that changemakers could be anywhere.

• Championing Changemakers (Chapter 8)

- Leadership development must be sponsored by the CEO and the leadership team.

- Development must be largely 'on the job'.

- Using changemakers from across the work domains effectively eliminates the need for expensive change programmes or consultants.

• Reward (Chapter 9)

- Problems with equity, and internal equity in particular, can undermine everything.

- Looking at reward through the lens of complexipacity ensures a common frame of reference when it comes to matching the job, the person and the reward.

- Reframing most pay issues as opportunity issues puts internal development at the heart of the solution.

Conclusion

I will close with my personal journey, outlining the significant impact the complexipacity assessment had on my overall confidence levels and the shape of my career thereafter.

Most of my development occurred while working for an organisation I absolutely loved and where I was a great culture fit. I felt privileged to have the position of head of HR and training in the organisation and had no aspirations beyond the role as I felt I had reached my level. I worked for a great functional boss who, lacking an HR background, involved me in everything (which I appreciated). I was happy to do all the work, assuming that I was getting the credit for my contributions.

When our MD suddenly changed, my boss left and to save payroll it was decided not to replace him immediately. Some six months later, my MD commented that he was rather perplexed by the situation in HR, as he had not noticed any decline in the function's output. It was at this point that he realised I had been doing a lot of the work and I realised that it had gone unnoticed until this point.

It was around this time that the MD challenged the lack of rigour in our own process to identify our high potentials. Specifically, he was fixated with the lengths of everyone's runway. Keen to provide a solution, I discovered the work of Elliott Jaques, Gillian Stamp and Sheila Rossan and was introduced to complexipacity assessments. Both the MD and I completed an assessment in order to personally experience the science for ourselves.

The conclusions that were drawn blew me away, with the output suggesting that I was more capable than I realised. Moreover, it suggested that I should actively consider asking for the HRD role, something that I had not considered. I distinctly remember the impact – I forgot to pick my children up from nursery that day as I was in such a daze!

The matter of a permanent replacement then came to a head. Asking me why he should give me the job, I explained that I had been doing it anyway, but more importantly, because the assessment suggested I could actually do it. The rest, as they say, is history but the combined impact of the confidence derived from the assessment and an MD who got to the nub of who was doing the work and then backing his internal talent creates valuable lessons and learning. I am convinced that had there not been a period of extended sick leave and my boss had just resigned an external would have been hired, and I think if you put my ex-MD on the spot he would say the same.

I was lucky. I had both a supportive boss and the confidence gained from undertaking a complexipacity assessment. On reflection, the assessment was one thing but all the confidence in the world still needs a boss prepared to take a chance on you. He would say that by completing the assessment he had underwritten and de-risked his decision.

9/11 followed soon afterwards, and with some external support because we were so new to the concepts, we put complexipacity at the heart of our UK turnaround strategy, driving our reinvention and new normal firmly through the people agenda.

The pressure is on and businesses need to:

- Reset, reinvent and build in the resilience to weather unanticipated storms.

- Address the rapid progress in technology and automation.

- Improve diversity at the top, answer questions over boardroom pay differentials and satisfy a challenging and vocal millennial workforce.

This can all be achieved by putting human capital right at the heart of business strategy. It is people that drive the culture, people that create products and services and people who enable the technology. The case for The Changemaker Effect has never been stronger. Unleash your organisation's potential and learn more about using 'The Changemaker Effect' proprietary methodology by contacting me at www. thechangemakereffect.com.

Acknowledgements

There are so many people who have supported and encouraged me to write this book. Special acknowledgements go to the following:

- Peter Duff, chairman at Shoosmiths, for your ongoing support helping me to convert the science into robust business and people outcomes.

- Phil Crowe, employment law partner at Shoosmiths, for all those insightful discussions on the significance of the work when applied to performance management.

- Peter Riordan, retail and property director, for allowing me to implement this work wherever we have worked together. It has generated some lovely stories, many of which are featured.

Additionally for your patience and dedication to reading and rereading the book time after time as it evolved.

- Scott Lanphere, Chairman of Omnio Holdings SA and TLNT Holdings SA, Managing Director of AEDC Capital Ltd and Eton Gate Capital Partners Ltd, for the opportunity to apply the work across your existing high-growth technology investment portfolio and to prospective mergers and acquisitions.

- Alex Didymiotis, group HR director at TFG (Phase Eight, Whistles and Hobbs), a fabulous example of how a changemaker can reach the top with the right CEO sponsorship. Well done for leading by example and sponsoring TFG's changemakers to such great effect.

- Melanie Reece, mentor in residence at Centrality's Blockchain Incubator (Auckland) for the opportunity to apply the work to make better early stage investment decisions.

- Dr Sheila Rossan and Peter Taylor, the managing director at Bioss UK, who have both patiently tutored me in the science.

The Author

In her early HR career, Jo always liked to be in the action and on the shop floor with customers and frontline staff. Feedback would consistently cite her ability to build strong relationships with line management, aided by her northern no-nonsense straight-talking style. Helping to diagnose the problems and then being available to support the line manager to resolve them was the key.

This enthusiasm continues to underpin her work, but it is the knowledge and experience of applying the science combined with her highly capable people management skills that make the real difference. Having Jo around as a strong support is always comforting when working through tough but necessary people decisions, whether as a CEO, director, manager or investor.

In Jo's latter corporate career, she worked most successfully in transformational turnaround projects where the science could have its maximum impact. She was then introduced to a couple of entrepreneurs and was intrigued to be granted the opportunity to apply the science to high-growth technology start-ups looking to scale – setting things up correctly from the start rather than always putting things right. Jo soon realised that in the start-up world the human capital piece is overlooked in favour of the product and/or the technology and has relished the opportunity to address this imbalance.

At a higher level, Jo's interest is in solving the problem of inequality of employment opportunity. Putting complexipacity at the heart of this problem has the power to transform individuals, organisations, communities and nations.

Outside work Jo is a passionate advocate of CrossFit and a qualified coach.

You can connect with Jo at:

🌐 www.thechangemakereffect.com

𝕏 @TheCMEffect

🔗 jo-steen-bb03b64

Printed in Great Britain
by Amazon